The Family Circle Dictionary of Antique Metals: Silver, Pewter, Brass, Copper and Iron

By Wendell Garrett
Editor of the magazine Antiques

Illustrations by Helen Disbrow

Ajouré. Metalwork which is pierced through, perforated or openworked for decorative purposes.

Alms Dish. A large dish on which church offerings were placed for consecration; usually of brass, but occasionally of silver.

Apostle Spoons. Spoons made with handles which memorialize the 12 Apostles. In the 16th century they were often given by godparents to a child at his or her christening. New versions and revivals were made into the 19th century. Apostle spoons are collectors' items today, especially as a complete set.

Aquamanale. A metal ewer or jug, often in an animal shape, used for washing hands during meals or for liturgical purposes.

Argand Lamp. A type of oil lamp invented by Aimé Argand, a Swiss, in 1783. A glass chimney protected a tubular wick, thereby increasing combustion because the air currents were contained.

Argyle. A silver pot, with a handle and a spout like that of a teapot or coffeepot, for keeping gravy warm, deriving its name from the 4th Duke of Argyll, who is thought to have introduced it. An encircling space was designed between the inner container and the outer wall to contain hot water. Argyles were common in the late 18th, early 19th centuries.

Assay. The process of testing metals, especially silver and gold, to determine their purity and quality. In the 18th century, if a piece of wrought silver plate was found to be below the legal standard, it was cut or battered and returned to the maker.

Assay Cup. A small cup, known also as a cup of assay, generally in gold or silver and used in great households by a trusted—and obliging—servant to sample his master's wine as a precaution against poisoning. Later versions were in the form of diminutive two-handled cups and used as wine tasters.

Astral Lamp. A form of Argand lamp, developed by Count Rumford, with a flattened ring-shaped reservoir for oil, which produced light without casting a shadow. Widely used in the 1830's and 1840's.

Bacon Dish. An oblong covered dish, generally in silver, fitted with a hot-water compartment.

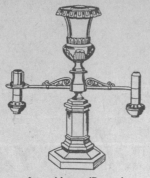

Argand Lamp (Bronze)

Bail (Brass)

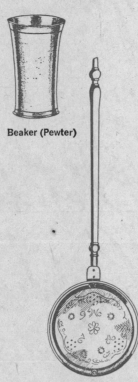

Beaker (Pewter)

Bed Warmer (Brass)

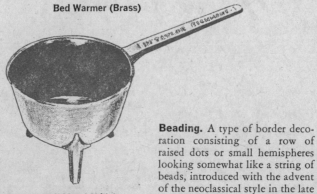

Bell Metal Skillet

ILLUSTRATIONS BY HELEN DISBROW

Bail. A drawer pull consisting of a curved piece of brass or bronze bolted at each end, and usually backed by a decorative plate. The bail handle superseded the drop handle and was very commonly used in the 18th century.

Baluster Measure. A pewter cup used for measuring liquids from a quarter of a gill to a gallon.

Baptismal Basin. A shallow silver or pewter vessel used for the rite of baptism. Many forms were made, some with a wide brim and some mounted on a low foot. Baptismal basins are a common form in American silver.

Basin. A container for water in which the hands were ceremoniously washed before and after meals. Before forks became widely used after about 1660, it was the custom to eat with the fingers. At the end of a meal, a basin and ewer were brought around by a servant so that diners could wash their hands and clean their teeth with a napkin dipped in the water. After the general adoption of forks, basins ceased to be used in this practical way. However, they continued to be made as presentation pieces, their purpose being chiefly ostentatious.

Basket. A silver form introduced in the 17th century for serving sugar and sweetmeats, bread and and cake. The term "basket" was applied because of the pierced or openwork decoration and because they frequently had arched swing handles. Some of this decoration consisted of fairly simple palings, occasionally with a slight Gothic flavor, but it sometimes included typical neoclassical elements such as swags and medallions.

Basting Spoon. A large spoon with a long handle and large bowl, used as a serving spoon. The long handle enabled the server to reach inside a cooked bird for juices and stuffing.

Beading. A type of border decoration consisting of a row of raised dots or small hemispheres looking somewhat like a string of beads, introduced with the advent of the neoclassical style in the late 18th century. It is found on the

edge and rims of plate of all kinds, including flatware.

Beaker. A large drinking vessel with a cylindrical body, widening from base to rim, with either tapering straight or concave sides and with a flat disk of silver forming the base of the receptacle. It was almost invariably supported on a molded foot-ring and might also have a narrow, molded girdle soldered around its middle.

Bed Warmer. A long-handled pan of brass, silver, copper or iron, with a perforated lid, used for live coals—or a similar flask-like vessel used for hot water. A heated bed warmer was placed between the bed sheets on cold nights to warm the bed, then withdrawn just as the person got in. Bed warmers represent such romantic notions of country life that many were reproduced in the 19th century for nostalgia rather than use.

Bell Metal. An alloy of bronze, copper, tin and zinc, used for casting bells because of its sonorous tone. Also used for making cooking utensils, especially mortars and measures.

Berry Spoon. A jargon name applied to a tablespoon or dessert spoon embossed from beneath the bowl with fruit ornament, and with the interior usually gilded.

Betty Lamp. A shallow, pear-shaped lighting device with a floating wick made of iron or tin that was used extensively in rural America into the 19th century.

Biggin. A percolator-type coffeepot invented about 1800 in England, possibly named after its inventor. The coffee was placed in a separate compartment in a vessel containing water.

Billet. The thumbpiece used to raise the lid of a tankard.

Bilston Blank. Tinware made in Bilston, England, and sent to other shops to be decorated; late 18th century.

Bleeding Bowl. A small, shallow pewter or silver bowl with a single pierced handle or lug, used for cupping or bleeding by surgeons when the supposedly therapeutic practice of bloodletting was popular. These bowls, which resemble porringers, are engraved inside with graduated lines to measure the number of ounces of blood taken from a patient.

Blowhole. A hole in cast work or solder caused by the escape of hot air.

Bobèche. The drip pan on a candlestick, large in size and located at the base during the 17th century; in the 18th century the bobeche moved up the baluster stem for stylistic reasons and was made smaller in diameter. By the early 19th century the small drip pan was placed at the very top of the stick.

Bottle Stand. A silver stand for a bottle or decanter, usually in the form of a shallow bowl. Popular in the 18th century and the ancestor of the coaster in the Adam period and later.

Bottle Tickets. Silver labels suspended round the necks of bottles or decanters by thin chains, engraved or pierced with the name of the contents—such as whiskey, gin, rum, brandy, shrub or strong ale.

Bouilloire. A French metal tea-kettle mounted on a spirit burner.

Brass. An alloy of copper and zinc.

Brass Furniture. A 19th-century furniture style that became popular with the Great Exhibition of 1851 in England.

Brasses. Cabinet hardware made of brass, including pulls, handles and escutcheons.

Brazier. A metal pan or bowl designed to hold burning coals or charcoal for cooking or room-warming purposes. In America, braziers were called chafing dishes. Later examples make use of lamps for burning spirits of alcohol with a variety of muffling devices.

Bright-cut Engraving. A type of engraving used on silver that differed from ordinary linear engraving in that shallow flakes or chips were removed from the metal by means of a broader-ended graver, so that the cut surfaces reflected the light. Applied to plate of all kinds, including spoons and forks, in the late 18th and early 19th centuries.

Britannia Metal. An alloy of tin, copper and antimony that is silver-white in color and essentially a very fine pewter as it contains no lead. Developed in England in the mid-18th century and widely used in America in the mid-19th century. It was also used as a base for electroplating in the 19th century.

Britannia Standard. The name for the higher standard of English silver that was compulsory for wrought plate from March 1697 to June 1720, and was indicated by

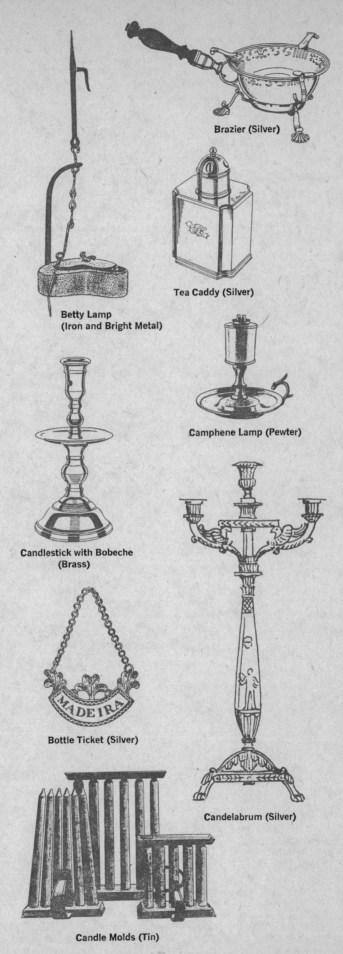

Brazier (Silver)

Tea Caddy (Silver)

Betty Lamp
(Iron and Bright Metal)

Camphene Lamp (Pewter)

Candlestick with Bobeche
(Brass)

Bottle Ticket (Silver)

Candelabrum (Silver)

Candle Molds (Tin)

a figure of "Britannia." The Britannia standard implied the presence, in 12 ounces of metal, of 11½ ounces of pure silver—as opposed to the 11-1/10 ounces of the Sterling standard. For reasons of expense and because the plate of a purer quality did not wear as well as sterling with a slightly higher copper content, the Britannia standard was no longer compulsory after 1720.

British Plate. An alloy, resembling silver, made between 1830 and 1855 and superseded by electroplate.

Bronze. An alloy of copper and tin especially suitable for casting because it expands slightly when first poured into a mold, forcing itself into every crevice, and then shrinks as it cools.

Caddy. A silver receptacle or canister for keeping tea. Whether octagonal, oval or rectangular in shape, nearly all were flat-topped with a central hole having a domed cover. Caddies were commonly made in sets of two or three, and were sometimes accompanied by a sugar bowl.

Caddy Spoon. A small silver spoon often having a fancifully shaped bowl and a short wide handle, designed to remove tea from a caddy and to be stored inside.

Camphene Lamp. A metal lamp, often of pewter, tin or Britannia ware, used in the mid-19th century for burning a mixture of turpentine and alcohol.

Can. A drinking vessel in a mug form with a single handle, like a tankard without a lid. The body shapes were varied—cylinder, baluster and cask—as were the hollow handles in both D-shapes and S-shapes. The typical can or mug had a bulbous-shaped body with a capacity of about a pint, was mounted on a circular base, and was fitted with a scroll handle with a thumb-rest at the top where it joined the body.

Candelabrum. A decorative candlestick with several arms, or branches, fitted to hold candles.

Candle Box. A tin box used to store candles, often designed to hang on the wall.

Candle Mold. A series of hollow metal tubes in a rack, designed to contain hot wax for candlemaking.

Cape Cod Lighter. A metal container in which a lighter of baked clay or other porous material on a metal handle was soaked in kerosene before being placed under firewood.

Cast Iron. A hard, brittle alloy of iron made by being cast in a mold, used for architectural and landscape elements, especially in the Victorian era.

Caster. A silver container for shaking sugar, pepper or other spices over food through a perforated, dome-shaped cover or lid. Often made in sets of three: one large (for sugar) and two smaller (for pepper and cinnamon or some other spice). The baluster shape persisted through the 18th century and was either polygonal or circular in section.

Caudle Cup. A two-handled cup, often with a cover, introduced in the 17th century for use in drinking caudle—a warm, thin, sweetened gruel mixed with spiced wine or ale.

Censer. A container with an open-work superstructure used for burning incense in religious ceremonies.

Chalice. A tall-stemmed silver or pewter wine cup with a shallow bowl, formerly used in celebrating the Eucharist. Such church vessels are today highly prized by collectors.

Chamber Candlestick. A low candlestick with a wide pan forming the base, and a scroll or loop handle fixed to the edge, designed to light the user's way to his or her bedchamber. Usually fitted with a conical extinguisher topped with a small knob finial, this type of candlestick was widely used in the late 18th and early 19th centuries.

Chandelier. A hanging, branched candlestick with multiple sockets; rarely of silver or pewter, more likely of brass.

Charger. A large platter or dish in silver or pewter, used especially for carrying meat to the table.

Chasing. A decoration on metal (particularly silver) made by raising or indenting the surface with a blunt instrument called a chaser.

Cheese Scoop. A long spoon with an ivory handle, having a bowl shaped like a half cylinder, and used for scooping cheese such as Stilton out of the interior of a wheel of cheese in order to preserve the outer crust. Late 18th and early 19th centuries.

Chocolate Pot. A vessel, similar to a coffeepot, used for serving hot chocolate. A removable finial on the top of the lid exposed a small aperture through which a rod was inserted to stir the contents immediately before pouring. This ensured that the skin that formed on the surface of chocolate was shared out among the company instead of falling to the lot of a single unlucky individual. A high-domed lid is a common feature on chocolate pots.

Chopin. A Scottish measure, often of pewter, for liquids; equal to 1½ English pints.

Cloisonné. A form of enameling in which delicate, ribbon-like pieces of metal are fixed onto a metal surface in the desired design to form compartments which are filled with enamel.

Coaster. A short cylindrical holder or stand for a decanter, usually with a turned wooden base covered underneath with baize and with silver sides. It enabled the decanter to be slid along the table without damaging the polished surface.

Coin Silver. American silver marked "Coin," from about 1830 to 1860, to indicate that the silver content was equal to that of U.S. coin—that is, 900 parts of pure silver out of 1,000.

Convoys. An old name for base or substandard metal added to a piece of plate in such a manner as to make detection difficult, with the fraudulent objective of increasing the apparent weight of the precious metal.

Copperware. Kettles, measures and other vessels of copper made by hammering a flat sheet of the metal over a shaped wooden block. Usually the hammering was continued until the hammer marks disappeared. Edges were joined by dovetails, fitted together and brazed. Engraved decoration on copper generally suggests a Continental rather than an English or American origin.

Coral and Bells. A silver whistle with bells and a coral stem for the entertainment of children; popular in 18th-century America.

Cream Jug. A silver container for cream that was introduced in the early 18th century. The first type had a baluster-shaped body with a scroll handle and was mounted on a foot-ring. Later examples of these jugs were pear-shaped and rested on three low feet, reminiscent of cabriole legs. In general, the styles of the body followed those of the teapot.

Cast Iron Cemetery Gate

Caster (Silver)

Chalice (Pewter)

Chamber Candlestick (Silver)

Coral and Bells (Gold)

Cream Pail. A silver form resembling a small pail, introduced in the late 18th century. Cream was served from it with a small ladle.

Cruet Stand. A silver stand designed to hold cruets, or miniature decanters, and silver casters for vinegar, oils and condiments for the dining table. In the rococo phase, these stands often had an applied asymmetrical frame for the owner's arms, crest or monogram. Introduced in the early 18th century, they were widely used in America in the 19th century.

Cut-Card Work. A method of decorating silver by cutting out shapes such as leaf forms from sheet metal and soldering them to the surface of the object.

Date Letter. A letter struck in alphabetical sequence (A to Z) on English silver plate after the assay and normally current for one year. Today, letters on a piece of English silver can be checked against standard tables of date letters to determine the age of the piece.

Door Knocker. A metal ring or hammer device attached to a door with a hinge. A common early form was the lion mask with a ring in the mouth. The more common dolphin-form knocker dates from the early 18th century.

Douter. An alternative to the extinguisher for putting out a candle, consisting of a scissor-like form ending in flat plates between which the wick was pressed.

Dram Cup. The name applied in America to a small, shallow, circular cup, often with handles, made for tasting wine or for taking a dose of medicine.

Drop. The reinforcing joint between the stem and back of the bowl of a silver spoon.

Drop Handle. A brass drawer pull in the form of a bulbous teardrop or pendant, in common use during the William and Mary furniture style (1689–1725).

Duty Mark. A hallmark, indicating the duty payment on British silver plate, in the form of the heads of successive sovereigns from December 1784 to April 1890 (that is, George III, George IV, William IV and Victoria).

Ecuelle. A French porringer or shallow bowl, generally with a dome-shaped cover and two flat, pierced handles. Ecuelles were introduced in the 17th century and made in England in the 18th century by immigrant Huguenots.

Egg and Dart. A type of repeating border ornament of classical design used on plate and consisting of rows of rounded convex moldings with arrowheads between them.

Electroplating. The technique of covering one metal with a thin layer of another by electrolysis. Copper, brass and bronze are still commonly plated with silver by this method which was patented in 1836.

Embossing. The art of producing figures or designs in relief on a surface.

Enameling. A method of decorating metalwork in which enamel (a form of glass) is fused to copper, silver or gold in a small kiln.

Engraving. A method of decorating the surface of silver with linear designs by cutting thin furrows in the metal with a graver or burin.

Entrée Dish. A covered silver bowl for vegetables, usually oval, oblong or octagonal in shape, and sometimes with removable compartments. Sometimes also fitted with a hot-water compartment or a spirit burner, or with a lid that can be readily converted into an extra dish.

Epergne. A decorative dining table centerpiece of silver consisting of a central dish or basket supported on a stand and several arms which support smaller baskets. Introduced in the mid-18th century.

Escutcheon. The decorative metal plate surrounding a keyhole, usually shield-shaped.

Etui. A small flattened cylindrical case with a hinged cover for needles, toothpicks and so forth; commonly in silver during the 18th century.

Ewer. A wide-lipped pitcher or jug with a handle, used for pouring wine or water and used along with a basin.

Fabergé. Gold and enamel miniature *objets d'art*—boxes, flowers, animals — made by a Russian jeweller and goldsmith of that name from 1870 to 1914; extremely valuable today.

Feather Edge. A narrow band of engraved oblique lines used to decorate edges of silver objects. Introduced in the second half of the 18th century.

Cream Jug (Silver)

Cruet Stand (Silver and Glass)

Door Knocker (Iron)

Dram Cup (Silver)

Fiddle Pattern. A handle form on silver forks and spoons which is fiddle-shaped in silhouette. Introduced sometime in the early 19th century.

Fireback. A cast-iron slab placed at the back of a fireplace to protect the brick wall and to reflect the heat. Often decorated with a date and molded design.

Fire Dogs. Andirons of a low, simple design. Fire dogs and andirons were used as early as the 16th century in royal households. Until the end of the 17th century, the uprights were heavily decorated; thereafter designs displayed greater sobriety, relying for their effect on satisfying forms and proportions rather than on surface decoration. Undecorated fire dogs were often made for kitchen use and were sometimes fitted with hooks for spits.

Fire Insurance Plate. A cast-iron decorative plate prominently displayed on the facades of urban houses in the Colonial period to indicate paid-up commercial insurance protection. In the era before municipal tax-supported fire companies, fellow insurees and delegated fire companies were obligated to assist in the event of a fire in any house bearing such a plate.

Fish Slice. A trowel-like silver object used to serve fish, introduced in the late 18th century. The form of the pierced blade and the handle varied: some were shaped like broad leaves, others were like builders' trowels, while those of the early 19th century were asymmetrical or in the shape of a fish, with openwork in the form of the backbone and ribs.

Flagon. A tall drinking vessel, usually of pewter, with a lid and a handle; a forerunner of the tankard. In churches a flagon was often used with a chalice.

Fluting. Decoration consisting of a band of narrow hollows with straight or sometimes curved sides, introduced during the Renaissance.

Foot Scraper. A metal device, usually affixed to a doorstep, for removing mud and snow from boots and shoes.

Fork. Forks were known in England as early as the 9th century, but did not become fashionable until after the restoration of the monarchy in 1660—even then their general adoption was resisted for many years. Early forks generally had two or more,

Fire Back (Iron)

Fire Insurance Plate (Iron)

Flagon (Pewter)

Foot Scraper (Iron)

usually three, prongs. In the third quarter of the 18th century, four prongs became more common. Patterns followed the contemporary profile of spoons; in the early 19th century the fiddle pattern was introduced from France.

Gadroon. A hammered or cast edge decoration for silver, consisting of a band or row of convex lobes separated by hollows and generally used around the foot of hollow ware; also known as *knurling*.

German Silver. An alloy of copper, zinc and nickel made to imitate silver but slightly more grayish in color.

Gilding. An ancient method of coating silver and other metals with a layer of gold. Pure gold was melted in a crucible with mercury, and the amalgam then painted over the surface of the object to be gilded. This was put over a fire, and the heat drove off the mercury in a highly poisonous vapor, leaving the gold permanently attached to the silver. Mercury gilding was the standard method until the introduction of the inferior, but safer, electro-gilding in the 19th century.

Gill. A liquid measure, often made of pewter, holding one-fourth of a pint.

Hallmarks. Marks introduced in England by royal decree in 1300, stamped onto silver and gold pieces when they were assayed by the craft guild, as a means of indicating quality and preventing fraud.

Hearth Broiler. A footed iron pan or grill used for broiling in an open hearth. Some pivoted to permit turning to face the hot coals.

Hollow Ware. All ware designed to be vessels or containers, such as mugs, cups, tankards, pitchers and bowls.

Hot-water Dish. A covered dish with a compartment into which hot water can be poured to keep food warm. In the 18th and 19th centuries, hot-water dishes had a practical purpose since kitchens were often located at some distance from dining areas.

Inkstand. A Victorian name for what was previously known as a *standish*.

Japanning. Decoration in black, red, and gold paint on tin in the Chinoiserie style, to imitate the

Gadroon Base Tea Kettle (Silver)

Hallmarks—19th Century (Silver)

Hearth Broiler (Iron)

Hot-Water Dish (Pewter)

Marrow Scoop (Silver)

Measure (Pewter)

more expensive lacquer work from the Far East.

Keyhole Pattern. An openwork pattern used widely on porringer handles; one of the openings resembles a keyhole.

King's Pattern. A 19th-century English silver pattern featuring a shell motif enclosed in a scroll design; similar to the Queen's pattern but more ornate.

Ley. A poor grade of pewter consisting mostly of lead and antimony and containing relatively little tin.

Liner. A container, often of blue glass, made to fit the interior of a silver object to prevent corrosion. Commonly used with silver mustard pots and salt cellars.

Loving Cup. A general term for a two-handled cup of any kind used by two or more persons who pledged each other from the same vessel in turn.

Marrow Scoop. An implement with a trough-shaped end or ends for extracting marrow from bones. Most examples are double-ended for bones of different sizes, with one end smaller than the other. Introduced in the late 17th century.

Measure. A metal vessel made to a standard size and used in retail trade for measuring liquids; sometimes stamped with its capacity. Measures came in sizes from ½ gill to a quart.

Meat Dish. An oval silver dish for meat with shallow grooves in the bottom to allow juices to drain into a deeper well.

Monteith. A punch bowl with a scalloped rim, made to hold iced water for cooling wine glasses that were suspended by their feet from indentations in the rim. Introduced in the late 17th century and named for a Scotsman who wore a cloak or coat with a notched hem.

Mote Skimmer. A strainer spoon with a pierced bowl and a stem terminating in a spike; used to remove leaves from the surface of a cup of tea and to free the strainer at the inside of the base of the teapot spout.

Mount. A piece of decorative hardware used on furniture, usually made of bronze, brass or *ormolu*.

Muffineer. A tall container with a perforated top used for sprin-

kling sugar or spices on hot buttered muffins; the same as a caster but smaller in size.

Noggin. A small cup or mug, often brass, sometimes with a face or head cast on. Also, a small amount of liquid equal to about one gill.

Ormolu. An ornamental wash made of ground gold or imitation gold used to gild the brass or bronze mounts on French 18th-century furniture and on Empire and Victorian revival furniture.

Pap Boat. A shallow 18th-century silver vessel designed for administering semiliquid food to infants and invalids. It is oval in shape, with a pouring lip at the narrower end and with neither a handle nor feet.

Pap Spoon. A pewter or silver spoon used to feed infants, generally having an elongated bowl partly covered with a lid hinged in the middle.

Paten. A miniature dish, usually in silver gilt, used for administering the sacred wafer to communicants in church.

Pewter. An alloy of tin mixed with lead, copper, brass, bismuth, zinc and/or antimony, shaped in molds or hammered into a variety of ecclesiastical and domestic forms of both hollow ware and flatware. Along with earthenware, pewter was in constant use in all but the most isolated frontier settlements and the richest coastal mansions. Most extant examples date from the mid-18th to the mid-19th centuries.

Pierced Work. A method of decorating silver and plated pieces by stamping or using a small piercing saw.

Pint Can. A standard-size drinking vessel, often of pewter and sometimes of bell metal, used in taverns in the 18th and early 19th centuries. Made to a full pint measure and so marked, it ensured the drinker's getting his money's worth.

Pipe Tongs. Miniature tongs used for lighting a pipe with a burning ember.

Plate. A synonym for silver. In modern times, an unfortunate practice has developed of using the term incorrectly for what should properly be called *plated ware*.

Plated Ware. Forms made of a base of copper or other metal

Monteith (Silver)   **Standing Salt (Silver)**

Pap Boat (Silver)

Porringer (Silver)

Pint Can (Pewter)

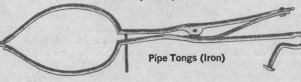

Pipe Tongs (Iron)

Sauce Boat (Silver)

covered with a thin coating of silver. From the 1740's until the mid-1800's, the metals were fused in a manual process, which was replaced in the 1840's by chemical electroplating.

Plateau. A long, low platform in silver with rounded ends, mostly supported on many small feet, running down the center of a dining table of the late 18th and early 19th centuries for candelabra and a centerpiece.

Pointillé. A method of decorating pewter by pricking it with a sharp pointed tool.

Pontypool. A town in Monmouthshire, England, where japanning on sheet metal originated; also a generic term for japanned articles in tinware.

Porringer. A shallow bowl of pewter or silver, generally with one flat, openworked handle but sometimes with two. Porringers were made in several sizes and were used for eating soup or stew.

Pounce Box. Pounce was a powdered resinous substance used to prevent ink from spreading on unsized paper. The design of the box —in silver, pewter or brass— generally conformed to that of the ink pot or standish.

Queen's Pattern. A 19th-century English silver pattern consisting of a shell motif enclosed in a scroll, or sometimes a fleur-de-lis motif.

Quaich. An 18th-century Scottish drinking or eating vessel, flat and shallow like a porringer, with a pair of horizontal handles attached at the rim.

Raising. The shaping, by use of a raising hammer, of hollow vessels from flat sheet silver. The silver is held at an angle against a polished steel stake and hammered down onto its surface, being rotated after each stroke. The stake, which is often shaped like the letter "T," is fixed into a section of tree trunk called a steady block.

Rat-Tail Spoon. An early type of spoon in which the handle or stem is extended under the bowl in the form of a tail to provide extra strength.

Repoussé Work. A type of ornamentation for copper, silver and gold that is raised in low relief from the back by using a hammer and punches of various shapes.

Rolled Rim. A curved tray edge formed by rolling over a wire.

Salt. The term for salt cellar, used into the 18th century. Most salts were in the form of a shallow bowl, sometimes on a circular foot and sometimes mounted on three or four small feet. They were decorated with applied leafage or pierced with classical or rococo forms, or with Chinoiserie, and fitted with blue glass liners. The earlier, massive standing silver salt container was placed at the center of the table (hence, the term about ranking at table, "below the salt"). American examples are often in the form of an octagonal-based pedestal, topped with a bowl-shaped indention and four scrolled brackets for the support of a plate or napkin.

Salver. A tray or plate on which food or drink was presented to a person, generally having a flat circular top mounted on three or four small feet arranged around the edge.

Sauce Boat. A silver vessel, usually elongated or boat-shaped, used to serve sauce for meat, fish or dessert. Generally there is a wide lip on one side, and a handle in the form of a vertical loop that curves outward from the rim and rejoins the body lower down. At the end of the 18th century, a covered sauce boat shaped like a miniature soup tureen in the form of a low, wide urn mounted on a short stem and foot became fashionable.

Saucepan. A pan used for "burning" the brandy used in the preparation of punch, sauces and the like. The majority had bellied bodies and straight, baluster-turned wooden handles. Examples dating from the early 18th century are expensive, and it is difficult to believe that they were relegated to the kitchen for ordinary culinary operations.

Scroll Handle. A handle—usually on hollow ware—shaped like the letter "S," with the lower half smaller than the upper.

Sheffield Plate. Articles made of a sheet of copper sandwiched or fused between two thin sheets of silver; a process invented in 1742 by Thomas Boulsover and developed in Sheffield, England. All kinds of plate were made in the 19th century, but Sheffield excelled particularly in the production of candlesticks. Once thin bars of silver were fused to the thicker bars of copper, the bars were passed through a rolling mill to flatten them into sheets which then could be hammered into the desired shapes by raising. Objects made of Sheffield plate followed the styles of contemporary silver; its manufacture declined steeply after the introduction of electroplating.

Snuffbox. A small box, often made of silver or pewter, used for carrying ground tobacco (snuff).

Snuffer. A scissor-like instrument made for trimming the wick of a candle. The term is widely misunderstood and misused, many people being under the impression that snuffers were used to extinguish candles. In the 19th century, wicks began to be made with a tighter thread on one side, causing them to curl over so that the carbon of the burnt portion disintegrated in the flame. But prior to this, the exposed part became longer as the wax or tallow was consumed and the wick was liable to bend suddenly downward and melt a vertical hollow in the candle with the attendant risk of fire. The snuffer often came with a tray on which later examples of snuffers rested on three small feet.

Spout Cup. A silver two-handled cup with a spout which rose from the base to about the level of the rim; probably used by invalids. Most date from the 18th century.

Stamped Work. A method of producing decoration by stamping silver with dies, or hammering it from the reverse side into hollow matrices.

Standish. The original name for what became known as an inkstand in the Victorian period. In the 18th century, the open tray design assumed a fairly standard form which lasted for most of the century. There is a socket for the inkpot at one end and another for the sandbox or pounce box at the other. The space in the center might be occupied by a taper stick, a box for small wafers for sealing letters or a silver bell. The inkpot often had holes around the top in which pens could be placed, although in some there is a long, narrow recess in the tray for pens, or a pen drawer underneath.

Sterling Standard. A term denoting the existence of 11-1/10 ounces of pure silver in 12 ounces (Troy) of metal, the remainder being copper.

Strapwork. Ornament, usually made by chasing or engraving, in the form of closely spaced parallel lines arranged in various designs.

Sucket Fork. A silver utensil, used for preserves and other sweets

Snuff Box (Gold)

Snuffer (Iron)

Wrought-Iron Latch

Surveyor's Compass (Brass)

Standish (Silver)

Tankard (Silver)

Pear-Shaped Teapot (Pewter)

Toaster (Iron)

Tobacco Box (Silver)

served in syrup. It had a two-tined fork at one end and a spoon at the other.

Sugar Sifter. A small ladle with a pierced bowl used for sprinkling sugar over food.

Surveyor's Compass. A precise mechanical tool of brass with sights, magnetic needles and an attachment for showing compensating adjustments for magnetic variations. In the late 18th and early 19th centuries, surveyors used these compasses in laying out the rectangular land divisions that form the continuous grid of farms, ranches and parallel roads from the Alleghenies to the Pacific.

Tankard. A drinking vessel, often of silver or pewter, with a single handle and a hinged lid. About 1700, a low dome on the lid began to replace the flat top that had been fashionable through the 1600's. The baluster shape was also introduced about this time and usually had a narrow molding applied around the most protuberant part. These curved baluster bodies were often accompanied by double-scroll handles. In the late 18th century, tankards were made in a cylindrical or cask shape. They were often engraved with vertical lines suggestive of barrel staves, and two sets of hoops were sometimes represented by engraved lines or applied bands. The lid was made of flat sheet silver and the hinge consisted of a riveted pin passing through a flange on each side of the handle. They were common until the Regency period, when silver tankards began to decline in popularity.

Taper Box. A cylindrical silver or pewter box with a handle like that of a miniature tankard; designed to hold a coil of taper or wick that emerged through a hole in the lid. The taper was lit to melt wax used for sealing letters.

Taper Stick. A holder for a taper in the form of a miniature candlestick, used primarily to furnish a source of flame for melting sealing wax.

Tappit Hen. A Scottish term for a pewter drinking vessel of various sizes, having a cylindrical body, a concave middle, a handle and sometimes a lid.

Teapot. A container with handle and spout in which tea is brewed with water that has already been heated in a teakettle. A mid-17th-century teapot was tall, with a

tapering body. In the late 17th century a shorter pot with a swan's-neck spout was used. The pear-shaped teapot dates from the 18th century, as does the globe-shaped teapot having a flattened top and footed bottom. Classical styles influenced the late 18th-century pots, when oval and octagonal forms were in vogue.

Threading. One or two narrow stamped decorative lines following the borders of various kinds of silver objects, particularly spoons and forks.

Tinware. Objects made from thin sheets of tin-plated iron. The pieces were often brightly painted with flowers, fruits, birds, portraits, landscapes and borders. (*See also* PONTYPOOL *and* TÔLE.)

Toast Rack. A silver or plated rack, introduced in the 18th century, used for serving toast at the dining table.

Toaster. An iron utensil consisting of a handle and frame for toasting bread on the hearth.

Tobacco Box. An oval silver or brass box with a loose lid, made to hold tobacco; introduced in the 17th century.

Tôle. The French term for painted tinware; that is, the French equivalent of *pontypool*.

Touch. The hallmark or maker's mark stamped or incised on a metal object; also the process of applying the mark.

Trencher Salt. A small, open silver salt cellar or dish placed near each person's trencher or plate.

Troy Weight. The system of weighing precious metals. As opposed to avoirdupois, the Troy pound contains 12 ounces instead of 16; the Troy ounce is divided into 20 pennyweights.

Wafer Box. A small box, generally of silver, designed to contain colored disks used to seal letters.

Wine Taster. A shallow silver bowl with a ring handle, used by vintners for sampling wine. The center of the bottom is often dome-shaped.

Wrought Iron. A type of iron containing very little carbon and some slag that is pliant enough to be drawn and hammered by a blacksmith at a forge. Commonly used for hardware, fences, grating and architectural decoration. ∎

SOUTHERN ANTIQUES

SOUTHERN ANTIQUES

BY

PAUL H. BURROUGHS

INTRODUCTION BY ELIZABETH HATCHER SADLER

BONANZA BOOKS • NEW YORK

PREFACE

OVER three thousand people lived on Virginia soil as early as 1620, and were a self-supporting group. Much of the furniture antedated by many years any permanent settlement made in New England or elsewhere. In the light of it, it is amazing that no study has been made of this craft and that almost no mention of it has appeared in what students of furniture making have had to say about early American furniture. Particularly is this to be wondered at with delay serving more and more to make the path obscure when such rich fields for research and study remain of a quaint and unique civilization, portraying itself in individual order and design.

The question of the origin of early Southern furniture is one that has been far too easily disposed of by students of American furniture making. The oft repeated announcement that "Southern plantation owners were in touch with the mother country and imported their furniture from England," does not cover the case. Even indifference in the South, and, everywhere, this lack of any real understanding of what was the case has prevailed; and I have long felt that some study was badly needed in the general field. The importance of this need has been borne in upon me more and more, as in my searching, more and better types have come to my hand. The furniture, itself, as pictured in this book and the facts that I am presenting, seek to tell the story as it is.

The quest for a Hepplewhite sideboard in South Carolina, where it was known they were to be found in abundance, may be said to have served in some degree to open up this vein of interest for me; and the difficulties under which I labored in an effort to locate that particular piece so impressed me that they, too, have not been without their influence in this book. The type of sideboard which I sought had been designated for me as shown in a book on antiques, but so ill-suited was the information available on the subject there or elsewhere, that before the search was abandoned my ideas on the type of book needed for the practical use of collectors was largely defined.

With so much wealth in the South, and money and tobacco leaving the hands of the planters so freely, many questions have presented themselves to my mind. I was asking, in particular, whether apprentices of well-known English and Northern craftsmen, when leaving their masters to seek their fortune—as apprentices did when their trade was perfected—did not come into the South as settlement proceeded, to follow their vocations in the rich and growing communities rather than continue in employment as they were, or set themselves up in competition with those under whose tutorage they had worked. Abundant evidence has revealed that many craftsmen came into the Southern colonies, and produced work there of a quality comparable with the best made in America.

No man stands out for producing exceptional types; but constant association and research bring out the salient points of the furniture they made. I have secured the names of more than seven hundred cabinetmakers in the South from 1737 to 1820, some of them working over a period of twenty years.

The furniture of the majority is what this book is concerned with. I have not tried to present the most elaborate nor the plainest example that is to be found, but have sought rather to show a representative piece, chosen because it is a Southern antique and of a type being found by dealers and collectors. Genius crops up in hidden places, and many unique and excellent pieces herein illustrated were made by unknown hands. Some pieces shown are unusual specimens, unattainable, and highly guarded in museums and private collections, and not the average of what the collector might be able to discover and become possessed of. There is charm, of course, connected with elaborate pieces representing large values, but the furniture of the South of the period covered by this book is not generally expressed in such rare examples. I am offering here what is typical, rather than the rare.

No attempt has been made to gloss the types, and the examples in this book are presented as found. The aim of the study has been to unearth the representative pieces. It has not been possible to present elaborate pieces, such as those made at Philadelphia by Randolph, Gostelowe and Savery, but each piece for consideration must, of course, have had merit of its own, and more and more has the study revealed that the individual artist at work can often produce results unattainable in the shops of the more expert craftsmen.

In making presentations in this book, conclusions have been reached after closest scrutiny and consideration. Opinions, in some instances, where available, have been called in. Besides proof afforded by the general situation affecting each particular case, judgment has been based on the quality of the particular type, and the fact that this type has been seen nowhere else has operated as a major influence. In all cases where Southern pine is used in construction, it has been assumed that it could not have been made anywhere else, and in the case of furniture made of curly cherry, it has been accepted as coming from in and around Winston-Salem, North Carolina, and as made by the Moravians.

With exception of four pieces only, what has been actually seen is shown here, and was personally brought to light, or seen in dealers' and collectors' public and private collections.

I am offering some pieces with labels, yellowed by age, as silent witnesses of authenticity, but with no idea of pressing the importance of the label itself, recognized generally as it is, that leading American cabinetmakers did not always label their pieces, and that the labels of many of them that did, have long since been removed in cleaning by the diligent Southern housekeeper or maid from the quarters at work, or by those attempting to refinish the piece.

I have been given valuable aid by the well-founded knowledge of many dealers and collectors. I wish especially to thank *The Antiques Magazine, The Antiquarian*

Magazine, Dr. Henry Berkley, W. S. Ahern, J. K. Beard, J. Pope Nash, Joe Kindig, Jr., and J. L. Roseman, together with many others living in the five states covered in this book, who have furnished information that helped in the preparation of the first book about Southern Antiques. If this effort to cover a large and interesting field serves in any way to stimulate others in the search for further data concerning the furniture craftsmen of the old South, then it will have fulfilled its mission.

PAUL H. BURROUGHS.

Richmond, Virginia,
    August, 1931.

PREFACE TO THE FACSIMILE EDITION

This pioneer work on early American furniture and its craftsmen, long out of print and very much sought after, is being reissued in a format as close to the original as possible, yet substantially below the premium it brought as a scarce collector's item.

The tremendous rise in the use and collection of antiques has heightened the interest of amateur as well as professional in the history and development of pieces made by early American craftsmen and, in particular, by those of our Southern colonies, where the pattern of gracious living flourished early in America.

To dispel the belief that affluent Southerners were in the habit of importing their furniture from England,

Paul Burroughs discusses the background and work of many of the more than seven hundred cabinetmakers who worked in the South from 1737 to 1820. A number of these started as apprentices in England and in the Northern colonies, and made their way eventually to the American South bringing with them the traditions and styles of the English master craftsmen.

The material here is fully as valuable today as it was when it was first published. The only standards that may not hold true today are the references to monetary offerings detailed in his chapter "Seeking Southern Antiques." Nonetheless, his experiences in locating interesting pieces could be shared by collectors today.

J.H.R.

CONTENTS

INTRODUCTION

MORE and more there is apparent in the heart of the nation an instinctive turning toward the South and what it has to offer by way of its past. Maryland, Virginia, the Carolinas, and Georgia call to mind a civilization on which the mind of America lovingly dwells, a group of early settlers whose memory is a matter of pride to their descendants scattered throughout the land, whose sacrifice, high thinking, and achievement is deep patterned in the upbuilding of the republic. Everywhere throughout this broad land of ours there is an instinctive groping for what remains of the beautiful and practical of that past.

SOUTHERN ANTIQUES presents examples of the work of Southern craftsmen done from the time when the country was young, beginning in 1620, when the life of the Virginia colony was getting well under way, and continuing through the pioneer period when Maryland and the Carolinas fell into line around the middle and late part of the seventeenth century, and when Georgia more than half a century later took up her task. This means not only the period of early pioneering and the gradual setting up of homes as the colonies expanded and population increased, with simple furniture everywhere the order of the day. It means, likewise, the period of furniture development in England and on the Continent, matching in time the struggles of the French and Indian wars here, the agitations and discontent preceding the Revolution, the war itself, and the period of the early Republic as influenced by English masters. The book extends on through to 1820 when the Empire influence dominated and when James Monroe, the last of the Virginia presidents, in the period of the Virginia ascendancy, was entering his last term.

A book about antiques, to be of value in collecting, must present something typical rather than elaborate and highly developed, and what is said must be said in terms within the limits of the understanding and opportunity of the average collector. His need is for something by which he may be guided in his search; and the information must be given in a manner intelligible to him, and not, as it is, often obscure for him by the use of technical terms known only in the parlance of the cabinetmaker.

Mr. Burroughs has made this book for the lay reader as well as the collector. Furnishing historical background pertaining to the settlement and general life of the period, it shows something of the rise and progress of Southern furniture making, and ties up the craft with general movements originating elsewhere. Types are presented with some study accompanying each piece, in the light of the period in which it was made, with general summaries preceding, showing the development of Southern furniture, considered class by class.

ELIZABETH HATCHER SADLER.

Careby Hall,
　　Fluvanna County, Virginia.
　　　　August, 1931.

I
THE FIVE COLONIES

THE settlement of Virginia is a tale too often told to repeat. Whoever may have been the first to reach the shores, it is with the coming of Admiral Newport that history chiefly concerns itself, heading as he did, a company from London, aboard the *Sarah Constant, Goodspeed,* and *Discovery.* They set their stakes about fifty miles above the mouth of the river which they called the James, and set about speedily at Jamestown to meet the requirements of living, as best they might, and here achieved the first successful settlement of the white man on the North American continent, making of the spot one to which all Americans turn with instinctive reverence and faith—the spirit of the undertaking there embyronic of what the spirit of the nation was to be.

As the colony grew, the pioneers setting up homes pushed inland along the Virginia rivers through Tidewater, the York, the James, and the Rappahannock, later into Piedmont. On they moved into the mountains of the Blue Ridge and the far country beyond, with Williamsburg, Norfolk, and Alexandria the leading ports of the colony, and Richmond, Charlottesville, Staunton, and Winchester making a later appearance.

Settlement was first accomplished in Maryland with the arrival of Leonard Calvert in the *Ark* and the *Dove,* in which he came westward, as sent by his brother Cecilius Calvert (Lord Baltimore), with perhaps twenty gentlemen and two hundred working men and servants, largely English,

to take possession of lands for which he held royal grant. In 1634 he sailed into the smooth waters of the Potomac, and pushed his way up the river to what is now Blackiston's Island, where he set up a cross at Saint Clements, later to fall back, however, seventeen miles down the Potomac near its mouth, to the site he chose for his capital; he called it Saint Mary's.

Much of the life of the colonist centered about the rivers. Along the James in Virginia, were scattered the homes of the planters, recalling the names of the Randolphs, the Byrds, the Carys, the Pages, too many to tell. William Randolph settled at Turkey Island, his descendants to scatter throughout the State along the river to Varina, to Tuckahoe, to Dungeness, and later, one of them along with Peter Jefferson to go to the mountain fastness of Albemarle, and open up the country where the Coles, the Rives, and others are found to this day. Williamsburg, settled in 1632, built itself rapidly and took a leading place in the life of the colony. It became the seat of the royal government, where William and Mary College was established, and where around its Palace Green and along Duke of Gloucester Street and elsewhere, homes of much excellence and finish were to arise, with furniture in keeping, to furnish fine background for the hospitalities they were to extend.

On the York, and on the Rappahannock at Corotoman, where lived King Carter, king of many lands; at Fredericksburg where Washington himself lived as a boy and where notables took quarter at the Rising Sun Tavern; at Rosegill, Sabine Hall, Mount Airy, and elsewhere were homes of splendor and charm, the master, himself, as well as his lady, a lover of fine trees, rare shrubbery and blooming flowers. There too, doorways flung wide, opening into paneled halls and showing furniture of distinction, either local-made or pieces of foreign importation, influencing that type which we seek in the South today.

On the Virginia side of the Potomac, with Alexandria as a center of trade and shipping, although each plantation maintained its separate wharf, as time progressed, little towns sprung up. On down the river, the homes of the planters increased, the list indeed a royal one, with the Washingtons first in Westmoreland on the Northern Neck, and George and Martha later at Mount Vernon; farther inland the Fairfaxes, George Mason among his books at Gunston Hall, and lower still, overlooking the river, Stratford, the home of the Lees. On the Maryland side, Marshall Hall; near by old Port Tobacco, Rosehill, Habre de Venture, home of Thomas Stone, the signer; La Grange, built by Doctor Thomas Craik; Mulberry Grove, home of the Hansons; Mount Victoria, Hard Bargain, Tudor Hall, Porto Bello, and Clocker's Fancy might be found.

Annapolis, having shaken itself into a dreamy existence on the banks of the Severn, with its quaint and winding streets, rare shops and homes of affluence, built in finest English style, where the Pacas, the Hammonds, the Chases vied with each other in the elegance of their surroundings,

became the center of business and social life of the colony. It was to lead in the making of Maryland furniture for years.

Maryland, a royal colony in close touch with the mother country, imported rare pieces which were often used for examples, and perhaps, more than any of the colonies, clung to the English ideas in furniture making. Life was lived at the best, and fine furniture was a necessity. Throughout the State might be mentioned other manor houses and settlements contributing to the general need: between the Patuxent and the Potomac, in Calvert and Anne Arundel Counties, Tulip Hill, overlooking the bay; Belair, with its wealth of fine furniture and other spots through Prince George, and the upper bay counties and finally, Baltimore, the Eastern Shore of Maryland, Kent County, Queen Annes, Talbot, Caroline, Dorchester, Wicomico, Somerset, Worcester, each with its share.

In Virginia, the Eastern Shore jutting almost into Maryland, Accomac and Northampton Counties, early opened up, where many relics of the past survive today, seems almost a part of it. Hand in hand, the two colonies, Virginia and Maryland— Leah and Rachel, they were called—moved together, bound by mutual ties of blood, descent and marriage, defense and material interest in commerce and shipping, with the Potomac, the theatre of mutual business and social pleasure, a dividing line that served rather to bring together than to set them apart.

That certain piece of land in 1663, lying between Florida and Virginia, was granted by Charles II of England to Lord Clarendon and a number of noblemen, and they proceeded to set up a proprietary government. English settlers from Virginia had already established themselves on the north of it, at Albemarle, at the mouth of the Chowan River in North Carolina, and in 1670 the earliest settlement of the southern part of this territory was effected on the banks of the Ashley and Cooper Rivers, under William Sale, to be moved in 1680 to the site of what is now the city of Charleston, South Carolina. There, with such inviting climate and fertile soil, newcomers were easily lured.

Governed though they were under one proprietary government, the two colonies remained separate and distinct, and grew in spite of difficulties between the people and proprietors, bent on serving selfish ends. The colony to the south, although much augmented in its population, was much retarded in its growth, due to dissatisfaction felt by the people with the governors sent them by the proprietors and the attempted enforcement of the laws of trade. Happily, in 1729, the two colonies were constituted each a royal colony—North and South Carolina. Complete separation was then established.

The population of this southernmost colony, South Carolina, soon assimilating itself, was composed of Englishmen of standing, English, Scotch and Irish dissenters, Dutch, Huguenots, Swiss, Quakers and Belgians. Too remote from the more northerly centers of population, she worked out her own fate largely alone, and cultivated her interest in England and the West Indies with the same interest if not more, than did those at Williamsburg or Annapolis, and maintained close relationship with the West Indies from whom so much of her population was derived.

Commerce, it has been said, was of noble origin in South Carolina. Despite the threat of pirates and the constant fear of Indians and Spanish and French to contend with on her borders, the colony on the Ashley prospered as the West Indian planters from early days cast their lot more and more within it, and the migration of French Huguenots, a steady and valuable one, continued. Due to the presence of many negroes, the plantations established within themselves such a highly organized plan as to create a system baronial in its sweep of power and influence. Plantation owners were often merchants and traders as well, and after the proprietary lord had been ordered to move his "Towne of Tradd" from Albemarle Point to the opposite peninsula, settlement throve and commerce walked with a high head through the winding streets of old Charles Town, building itself up into a rich city, with money enough not only to import luxuries but to attract high-class craftsmen as well.

A little more than one hundred years after the founding of the colony of North Carolina, her population numbered three hundred thousand people. They were English, Scotch, Swiss, Irish, and Moravians, and the mixing of these races has had a tendency to influence the design of furniture which they produced outside the larger settlements. In Mecklenburg County, and in and around New Bern and Edenton, as well as Raleigh, there is much extant of a highly picturesque past, showing remains of elegance in architecture and woodwork of unsurpassed artistry reflected in the making of furniture, which speaks for itself. It is recalled that at New Bern, John Hawks, from the Isle of Wight, and James Coor, whose work has been compared favorably with that of McIntyre, the master carver of Salem, did some of the carving and influenced, of course, the makers of furniture there, where unusual pieces are found today.

Contributing largely to the settlement of Virginia and North Carolina, and reaching into South Carolina, was an inland migration composed largely of Germans and Scotch-Irish, who took up their abode from time to time, as fancy moved them, in various settlements. Down through the Shenandoah Valley they came, on through the country of Winchester, Harrisonburg, Lexington, and southward toward Charlotte, even into South Carolina, carving out a destiny of their own, creating at times a unique civilization and leaving numberless witnesses behind in customs and traditions, old houses and furniture with marks of their own making upon them, as testified to in inventories and records. Much of this furniture, often pieces of worth, was made by the many cabinetmakers who made their way in and out of the various settlements in search of trade, as the small towns arose along the old post road.

A group of Germans, in America seeking opportunity for freedom in the exercise of their religion, followers of John Hus,

established in 1753 a Moravian colony at Salem (now Winston-Salem), in North Carolina, where they constituted themselves on arrival into a community, made laws unto themselves, and put their imprint on much that remains to us today, and particularly on the types of furniture which have been found.

Georgia was the last to be established of the English colonies, the first settlement made at Savannah, in 1733, under James Oglethorpe. The early colonists were Germans, Scotch, Swiss, Portuguese, and English, but the majority after 1752 came from the Virginia Cavaliers. Lord Oglethorpe came over with the idea in his mind in setting up a buffer State by way of protection of Carolina from the French and the Spanish, to the south and west, and in making the colony a retreat for those suffering religious oppression in England, and for others desiring to free themselves of debt, with various schemes for them proposed. Silk raising was to be cultivated as a means of livelihood, but all this gave way in time, and Georgia finally yielded largely to the same influences surrounding the other colonies. More closely tied up with the English, however, the majority of the furniture of worth found there has proved to have been imported, not only from the home country but from New England as well.

SOUTHERN CABINETMAKERS

PERHAPS there is no more pronounced instinct in the general character of the early Southerner than that of home-making. Scattered throughout this broad land today, are houses dating back to within a few decades of the first settlement of the white man on the North American continent, and there is much about them of beauty and comfort to impress the traveler. The fact is obvious that the best of the energies of these valiant and resourceful people were employed in surrounding themselves not only with what was comfortable and enduring, but with what was made for beauty as well.

The manner of living on the best of the plantations is reflected in the wonder of today: the fine sites on high hills overlooking winding rivers that the masters chose for their houses; their gardens with boxwood, guelder-rose and moss fringes left to tell the story; the broad sweep of the lawn revealed through rare trees; white-columned houses with doorways of Ionic or Doric entablature; silver-plated door knobs, red walnut panelings, stairways with precious carving, and exquisitely made chimney pieces, with an abundance of servants to keep bright the crested plate, the china from Canton, fine glass and best furniture from England, brought often to their doors on their own ships.

All of this speaks of a passion for beauty of the owner; but back of it were hardships which even those best provided for had to endure, and the necessity always to cope with conditions as they were. It was inevitable that, out of it something fine as well as useful in the way of furniture making must evolve itself in these five colonies, with a need so immediate, the demand so increasing, and much of the material and labor at hand so easily obtained.

There were four carpenters numbered among the "Gentlemen" company composing the Virginia colony the year following their first arrival. Scant equipment was allowed in the ships coming over for many years, and furniture sent from England could not of course have met the demand. In 1748 there were three hundred thousand people to be provided for in Virginia alone, at a time when she extended from sea to sea. Because of the western expansion of the colony, the small farmer class living inland grew so rapidly that Tidewater aristocracy was in danger of being overwhelmed. Such a vast number of people needed furniture and needed it badly, and despite what they had with them or what followed them over, at least one-half the population must have supplied themselves with furniture at hand. What we know of what was owned at the time is derived largely from wills and inventories of the wealthy planters, and we cannot be guided solely by them.

"If you could help me to a carpenter, a bricklayer or mason, I would willingly pay you somewhat extraordinarily," was the cry of William Byrd, who having made his arrival in Virginia somewhat late in the sixteen hundreds, was ordering such and other goods of quality by the first ship from home, as he proceeded to set himself up. Carpenters and joiners, so varied were the uses to which they were put, were always in demand, and with the joinery of the first simple furniture corresponding to that of the house, we must believe that the work of furniture building was largely in their hands, as the cabinetmaker slowly emerged.

So excellent was the work that some of the Southern craftsmen eventually performed, that in 1768 we find Abraham Pearce, a cabinetmaker and carver from London, declaring in the *South Carolina Gazette,* that he "executes every Article . . . in the most elegant and workmanlike Manner," and announcing that, "Orders from the Country or any of the Northern provinces will be punctually complied with."

Landing, as the pioneers did, on barren shores, with the necessity for home-building ahead, the activities and resources of every one of them was called into play, and in every group there was some one or two, at least, who must assume the rôle of carpenter, if not, in fact, already chosen directly with reference to that trade. Shiploads, coming from time to time, provided them more and more, as the colonies pushed inward to meet further emergency. Plantation heads in need of extra help often secured such assistance, though it was necessary on the larger plantations for a cabinetmaker of ability to be numbered among the retainers, with need to be supplied both in the manor house and at the quarters as well.

As time wore on, and cabinetmaking progressed, various types asserted themselves. There were men putting out pieces of high merit, who worked independently, maintained fine shops, and were in the market for skilled craftsmen and apprentices as well, furnishing themselves with the best woods, and in time importing mahogany from the West Indies. Journeymen cabinetmakers went from place to place, supplied private needs, often on the plantation, or in shops and with other cabinetmakers, performed the task set for them, and moved on to other fields as the call arose. Considering the calls made for them in the newspapers, whether "taylors," weavers, or barbers or not, these journeymen laborers were in much demand. "Journeymen Cabinet Makers who understand their Business will meet with good encouragement by applying to Edmund Dickenson," we read, for example, in the *Virginia Gazette,* of Williamsburg, just following the Revolution, "Two journeymen chair makers" are listed as wanted by James Shackelford at Hanovertown, Virginia.

Apprentices were often bound. "Joseph Fontaine of Charles City County binds himself as an apprentice to George Donald, Cabinet Maker of Richmond for six years to learn the trade of cabinet maker," is set forth in the *Gazette,* and again, to the same man, we read at another time that "John Scott, guardian of Joseph Scott binds sd. Joseph as apprentice to learn the trade of cabinet maker." As advertised in connection with the vendue of an estate in Anne Arundel County, Maryland, among the salable articles we find a "White male servant versed in making chairs, tables and desks." The indentured, as well as the slaves, were often called to the bench; and sorry fellows some of them were, to be sure, impressed into service as need would arise, and perhaps often none too much in love with the task. An old Virginia newspaper records the disappearance of Joffath Rainbird, "a cabinet maker and Joiner by trade in Charles County, Maryland, a smooth-tongued, infinuating Fellow and an Englishman born."

Two of them at a time took off from one of the Virginia plantations, Richard Kibble, "a fquat Fellow of a fwarthy Complexion," and Samuel Vlein, "fmall and thin." Vlein's clothes must certainly have betrayed him, "a little White Cloth Coat with Cape, a white Jacket flowered on the Breaft with green Silk, a white Linen Shirt, a black Wig, an old Hat, a Pair of red Camblet Breeches" and, not to mention osnabrigs, white stockings and old shoes. Kibble's was no better, "his coat a burnished color, green double breafted Jacket, a check'd Shirt, a red fpotted Silk Handkerchief about his neck, a black natural Wig, a good Hat with black Crape about it"; and to complete the picture, along with "greafy Leather Breeches," worsted stockings and good shoes, "there were many Letters and Figures on his breaft and left Arm . . . the End of his nofe turns up pretty much and he professes to be a Carpenter and Joiner by trade." Vlein and Kibble, both one-time convicts, joiners and carpenters by trade, God rest their souls.

By 1640 Virginia had almost fifteen thousand people, and the demand for furniture was steadily increasing. More than one family often lived under one roof; families were large, as a rule, and the door stood open for strangers and friends alike, at all

hours. The amount of furniture required rose as the standards of living advanced. Virginia looked out for herself in this, one of her major needs, and her county files reveal a host of men at work. The earliest cabinetmakers recorded were those at Jamestown, Williamsburg, and Yorktown. Norfolk, Fredericksburg, Charlottesville, Richmond, and Wheeling (now in West Virginia) had cabinet shops. Petersburg, Richmond, Blackstone, and Wheeling produced chairs from 1760.

One of the master designers of furniture in Virginia, perhaps, as time wore on, as well as in architecture, was Thomas Jefferson, whose experiences in Paris, Southern France, Italy, and England in the period of the classical revival of architecture and furniture, from 1784 to 1789, must have served him in good stead. Numbered among the books on the Monticello shelves was one entitled, in his manuscript catalogue, as follows: "Chippendale's Cabinetmaker's Designs. Fol. Gentleman and cabinet-maker's directory; being a collection of . . . designs of household furniture in the Gothic, Chinese and modern taste . . . (with) a short explanation of the five orders of architecture—3d ed London 1755."

One of Jefferson's notes, written while traveling in Europe, records a "Memorandum on a Tour from Paris to Amsterdam, Strasburg, and back to Paris," and describes "Dining tables letting down with single or double leaves," and shows a set of miniature drawings illustrating his ideas.

His outstanding design was, perhaps, the table on which he wrote the Declaration of

Independence. In writing young Coolidge, of Boston, recently married to Ellen Randolph, child of the heart of his old age, to whom he was presenting the treasure, he wrote, "Now I still happen to possess the writing box on which it was written. It was made from a drawing of my own by Ben Randall, a cabinet maker in whose house I took my first lodging on my arrival in Philadelphia in May, 1776, and I have used it ever since, it claims no merit of particular beauty. It is plain, neat, convenient and taking no more room on the writing table than a moderate quarto volume, it yet displays itself sufficiently for any writing."

Jefferson maintained his own cabinetmakers at Monticello, and no detail, we are told, was too small for his own supervision. He, himself, tells the story of the grief of John Hemmings, his henchman at the bench, over the loss at sea of a piece made at his bench. "That beautiful writing desk he had taken so much pains to make for you." A clock, and other things at Monticello, record the genius of the mountain sage and philosopher. Dinsmore, a carpenter, likely assisted in this work.

Some mention, too, must be made of Bucktrout, who is known to have supplied Councillor Carter, in 1772, with eight mahogany chairs, and whose advertisement in the *Virginia Gazette,* August 11, 1766, announces that "Bucktrout, Cabinet Maker from London on the main Street near the Capitol in Williamsburg, makes all sorts of cabinet work, either plain or ornamental in the neateft and neweft fashion . . . . N. B. Where likewise may be had the Mathematical Gouty chair." In 1770, two bedsteads likewise were supplied the Coun-

cillor by another cabinetmaker from Williamsburg, Atwell by name.

Dr. Henry Berkley lists cabinetmakers in Maryland from every section of the State, as advertised in newspapers or noted in directories or otherwise: numerous men in Annapolis and the Northern Neck, in old Londontown and Dumfries, ports of shipping now extinct; in Frederick and Hagerstown, on the Eastern Shore of Maryland, and many in Baltimore, between 1746 and 1820, three hundred men or more plying their art.

Gerrard Hopkins, advertising as early as 1767, supposed to have had his training with Robert Moore, in Philadelphia, son of Samuel Hopkins, of Anne Arundel County, held forth at the Sign of the Tea Table and Chair in Gay Street, Baltimore Town, "and working in mahogany, walnut and cherry, sold things" in the newest fashions of that day. He continued to work for many years, dying as the century came to a close.

The cabinetmakers working at Annapolis were all English born, or sons of English artisans, we are told. Westward, in the State, they were English or largely German. The Baltimore cabinetmakers composed a varied group, with English, Dutch, German, Irish, Italian, and French found among the number. Some of the French, possibly from San Domingo, and Italians had shops for twenty years, and were building furniture during that time, the Reverdy Ghiselin chairs in the Saint John's College Museum representing some of their work.

Although many outstanding pieces are shown in this book, as a result of the workmanship of North Carolina craftsmen, the names of the men do not appear, except in particular instances. In that section of the State settled by the Germans and Scotch-Irish, where it is known that shops were frequent along the post road, many journeymen traveled back and forth in employment of their trade. In Wachovia, the Moravian settlement, in North Carolina at Salem, now Winston-Salem, two names, Feldhausen and Ingebretsen, are outstanding.

When the purchase of ground had been arranged in London, and in 1753 the foremost of the settlers having received a blessing for the undertaking, were ready to mount their horses for Philadelphia, there to proceed South to undertake the establishment of a colony in North Carolina, where their ideals of living and the worship of God might find realization, these two men were among the number, having been selected particularly in regard to their trade. Heinrich Feldhausen, born in Holstein, listed as shoemaker, carpenter, millwright, turner, and Pennsylvania farmer, in his certification for Moravian membership, must have been something of a man. Erich Ingebretsen, just thirty-one, born in Norway, likewise millwright and carpenter, was by no means an inconspicuous person, becoming as he did later, single brothers' vorsteher, church warden, and vestryman for the Parish of Dobbs.

Down the Chesapeake to Norfolk the little company sailed, there to take horse and make their way to Edenton, and, on through Guilford County, to the point of settlement at Bethabara and Salem. Here it was that the big work of the two craftsmen began, with the brothers' houses to be built, equipment to be provided, as they took their places as pioneers in joinery, where other joiners arose to meet the need. A cabinetmaker before many years is mentioned at Salem.

In Georgia various cabinetmakers have been listed, and there were as many as thirty accredited to Savannah; but there is little evidence of any work of outstanding merit being done there by the local men, although the influences surrounding the craft around Savannah could not have been far removed from those at Charleston, with the same ships calling often at both ports. Atlanta, as well as Savannah, had cabinet shops by the end of the eighteenth century.

Advertisements appearing, mainly in the *South Carolina Gazette,* from 1732 on, reveal the working of an unusually active line of men carrying on a high-class trade, some businesses of long standing, men of various birth and extraction, putting out furniture of exquisite workmanship. No attempt will be made to call the long list of these worthies, though many names will appear from time to time in this book, the total number of them, so far arrived at, considerably exceeding two hundred.

Abraham Pearce, from London, carver as well as cabinetmaker, has been shown seeking to supply the Northern trade; and John Packrow, in 1764 announced that, having given over his business at Jacksonborough, "and carrying it on at the upper end of Tradd Street, he was returning thanks to his country and town customers for their Favours."

Cabinetmakers from England and the North found it profitable to set themselves up in towns throughout the South, and at

Charleston, as early as 1732, James Mc-Clellan, "cabinet maker from London," announced himself through the Charleston paper. In 1747 William Hizner, from Philadelphia, entered the Maryland field, Anderson, from Liverpool the year before setting up at Annapolis. In 1743 we read that William Lupton, "cabinet maker from London," was making himself available in Charles Town; Thomas Lining, five years later, "lately arrived from London," was announced. Robert Deans, "Joiner from Scotland," in 1750 made himself known. So they came: Richard Baylis from London, 1739, Hall from London, Mac-Grath, Fisher, Biggard from Philadelphia, and Warham from Boston.

Josiah Claypoole, in Charles Town, as early as March 22, 1740, from Philadelphia, is shown doing work of excellent variety, although none too well pleased at the treatment his fine furniture received at the hands of negro servants. He made desks and bookcases even at that early period, with arched pediments and ogee heads, evidencing the high character of furniture to which these craftsmen aspired, as shown by the following notice from the *South Carolina Gazette:*

"Notice is hereby given that all Persons may be supplied with all Sorts of Joyner's and Cabinet Maker's Work, as Desks and Bookcases, with Arch'd Pediment and O.G. Heads, Common Desks of all Sorts, Chests of Drawers of all fashions, fluted or plain; all sorts of Tea Tables, Frames for Marble Tables all after the newest and best Fashions and with the greatest Neatness and Accuracy by Josiah Claypoole from Philadelphia, who may be spoke with at Captain Crosthwaite's in King Street. . . . . N. B. He will warrant his work for seven years, the ill usage of careless Servants only excepted."

So much was foreign training taken as a matter of course, that Isaac Johns, according to the *Maryland Journal,* felt called upon to explain that although he "cannot boast of European education," he had "served his apprenticeship to William Moore in this town who has had long experience in the several shops in the principal towns of the United States."

Best wood, native and foreign, was supplied; books of design were available. Tools of all descriptions were advertised as imported, some even by Shaw and Middleton, at one time cabinetmakers and later importers as well. Locks and brasses were brought in. The outstanding influence, of course, on the general quality of what was made, were the examples of furniture of exquisite line that came into the South from elsewhere, however much they may have served to reduce the amount of furniture produced.

The Southern colonies were mainly English in settlement, and in close touch with the mother country, and the generally accepted theory is that much furniture was imported from Britain into the South. The contention cannot be denied. The plantation owners, largely of Cavalier extraction and connected by birth with well-established people in England, as the mode of living over there improved, were entirely without any other idea than that of keeping pace in their living, when possible, with their kinsmen abroad. So these lordly gentlemen were constantly directing their

agents, as has been pointed out, for dis-
posals of such funds as were placed in their
hands as a result of the sale of their tobacco,
cotton and rice, in plate and silver, china,
glass, rugs and furniture when occasion
demanded.

Importers, too, brought in rich goods.
Especially in Maryland, do we find them
listed as doing particularly good business.
Stephen West, of Maryland, lists at one
time, as from London, "household and
kitchen furniture of the very best kinds.
Beds and furniture, screens, mahogany
chairs, tables of all sizes, card tables, tea
tables, elbow chairs, tea boards, dressing
tables, carpets, looking-glasses, pewter
dishes," and other things, "all to be sold
very cheap." (1752).

Furniture, too, was brought South from
the North. The ship, *Sea Nymph,* of London, in 1739, according to the *Gazette* from
New England, coming into the York with
one dozen desks and one dozen tables along
with ballast. Drawers, fine desks, and other
things came aboard the sloop, *Ruth,* of
Rhode Island, the same year.

With factors from English merchants in
almost every port, inducements offered, and
the buying of foreign stuff made easy,
competition must have been difficult. "Any
person," declared one of the traders in
1731, in the *Virginia Gazette,* "who is in-
clinable to deal for a Parcel of Goods at
the Value of Three or Four Hundred
pounds may be supply'd Cheap for Tobacco, to be paid Time enough to be Sent
back Home by this year's ship." But the
local craftsman, undaunted, worked on,
not without inducements of his own to
offer, and his argument that home-pro-

duced furniture could be secured at less
price and in less time, was a sound one. In
marked confidence as to the excellence of
his work, he boasted outright that he was
not to be outdone.

Then, too, there was an ebb as well as a
flow in the tide of importation, particularly
as the colonists reacted in resentment to the
Stamp Act, and the further injustices put
upon them following its repeal in 1766.
When the next year, a new tax was put on
tea, glass, papers, and painters' material,
and the Townsend Act followed, imposing
other duties on tea and glass, sugar, lead,
and paper, the wrath of the colonists further overflowed. Charles Carroll, of Maryland, in 1768, in high feather, made his
wrath plain to an English friend, informing him by letter, of his confidence in the
ability of American craftsmen to produce
for the colonists anything which at that
time they were buying from England, which
they might choose to shut off.

"Every duty you send us Operates Ap-
parently as Bounty and Encouragement to
us to manufacture th^t species of goods."
American linens and woolens had received
a great boost on the passing of the Stamp
Act. "Surprising & astonishing was ye progress in Manufacture Here Especially in
the Woolen & Linnen Branches," he told
him. "The repeal of the Act gave a great
check to th^m . But they are reassured not
with a noisy & ostentatious Parade, But
wth a sullen Resentment & determined
Resolution never more to abandon th^m."
As for Gentleman Carroll, at the time of
the first excitement he had manufactured
"a Suite of Cloathes" for himself. "I wore

it to incite others to follow my Example" he continued; "I dropt my manufacture & laid aside my Cloathes upon the repeal of the Stamp Act. I have this year Built a Commodious House for as many Manufacturers as will be able to Cloathe between three & four hundred slaves."

Copies were made of best furniture imported, even that imported by so great a person as Peter Manigault, at the time of his death, one of the richest men in America, and listed as merchant, factor, trader, manufacturer and planter, who went to sea in his own ships, to England, the Barbadoes or North American ports. And one MacGrath was bold enough to believe that work that went out from his shop was of sufficient merit to be announced as following importations of the great Manigault into Charles Town.

In 1772 Richard MacGrath was offering goods which "he will engage to be as good as any imported from Europe and will sell them at the lowest prices for cash or short credit — Double Chest of Drawers with neat and light pediment Heads which take off and put on occasionally. Dining Tables; Commode Card Tables, Breakfast Ditto with Stretchers; China Tables; Sophas with commode fronts, divided into three sweeps which give them a noble look; carved chairs of the newest fashion, splat Backs, with hollow slats and commode Fronts of the same pattern as those imported by Peter Manigault, Esq. — He is now making some Hollow-Seated Chairs, the seats to take in and out, and nearly the Pattern of another set of chairs imported by the same Gentleman, which have a light, airy look and make the sitting easy beyond expression."

III

WOODS USED IN SOUTHERN FURNITURE

WOOD was the treasure of the early pioneer. Captain John Smith gave vent to his feelings in regard to the "oke." John Bartram, on a trip South, from Georgia, sent home accounts of his host squaring logs for shipment in cypress and in pine wood. Such *Virginia Gazettes* as are available, lift the curtain of the 1730's and reveal a busy fleet of small vessels clearing in the York and James for long voyages to distant ports. Bringing in such stuffs as Madeira, and sundry European luxuries, rum from the Barbadoes, negroes from New Guinea, and much else besides, they got away loaded with staves, hoops and headings, oak plank, and with much walnut, for England, where the quality was inferior to that the colonies produced.

The schooner *Grampus* cleared for Boston with corn, peas, wheat, and four hundred feet of walnut plank; a brigantine for Grenock, with tobacco and oak; the *Snow Kitty* and *Nora* for London, with tobacco, oak and skins; the *Staunton* for London, with "500 feet of Walnut Plank"; one with "Oak Boards" for Bristol; another with staves and headings for Glasgow; and the *Buchanan* out of the York with "Oak Board" for Antigua and Barbadoes.

Walnut, cherry, and pine were the woods most used by the early furniture makers of the South, until the advent of mahogany, when that wood, of course, went rapidly to a place of unquestioned supremacy. Virginia, from the earliest times, has been noted, as today, for its fine old walnut trees; and home-grown walnut, appealing to the luxurious, and used abundantly for paneling in Southern houses was, as a rule, the first choice of the Southern furniture builders for highly finished pieces. Due to its fine sheen and smooth grain, its other general characteristics which make it, today, often difficult to distinguish from mahogany, it did much to lift the general character of the work produced.

Early Southern pine, highly serviceable and lasting, and found in great abundance, was made use of for framing of furniture, and as a base for veneer. Oak, the king of woods, so thought, plentiful as it was, was little used, except in earliest times and after 1700, its chief employment was for the framework of larger pieces. Little maple or birchwood was used, except in the earlier days, and it went into disuse until 1800, although it grew in abundance. Poplar, almost as soft as pine, easily planed, was used extensively for drawer and side pulls.

Cherry, besides being popular in Annapolis, where both the wild and the cultivated was employed, was used in Maryland to a great extent, inland. From the earliest times, and up to the Victorian period, it was used particularly around the Moravian settlement at Salem, and red and white cherry is recognized in the majority of local-made furniture in the western part of North Carolina, as well as around the Moravian settlement. Many handsome

13

pieces are found with fronts veneered with curly or burl white cherry, which has a close resemblance to maple, with sides of red cherry resembling mahogany.

Mahogany was used as early as 1750, in Baltimore, and its advent into the United States, the best of it from the West Indies, the Santo Domingo, marked an era in furniture building here as elsewhere. Its virtues have ofttimes been listed: its strength and wearing qualities, its fine grain, its value as a veneer, the ease with which it is worked, the magic wrought from it in the hands of the carver, its susceptibility to polish and the sheen of it under stain— and Southern craftsmen rose to their best heights with this wood in their hands. Many fine inlaid Southern pieces of mahogany have been found in the vicinity of Raleigh, Greensboro, and Edenton; some around Norfolk, Charlottesville, and many, of course, in Maryland. Many advertisements, in South Carolina and elsewhere, offered mahogany furniture as the greatest of their achievements. In this connection, the *South Carolina Gazette,* of August 12, 1732, presents an interesting advertisement:

"At Newmarket Plantation, about a mile from Charles Town will continue to be sold all sorts of Cabinet Work, Chest of Drawers, and Mahogany Tables and Chairs, made after the best Manner, as also all Sorts of Peer Glasses, Sconces and Dressing Glasses. Where all sorts of Bespoke Work is made at lowest Prices by Mess. Broomhead & Blythe."

Maple, boxwood, holly, and satinwood were employed in the South for inlay, or sometimes, veneer, which after the advent of Hepplewhite, had some use. Pieces showing earlier use were imported.

It has been shown by Dr. Henry J. Berkley, of Maryland, that pine, yellow and white, was used there from the earliest times, for seats of chairs, legs and tops of tables, and common furniture, and used also with veneers. Hard, yellow pine was used for construction when not seen. White was also used in Maryland framing, as were ash, oak, and gum. Desks and cabinets, with frame wood bottom, and sides of drawers not covered with mahogany, cherry, or walnut veneer, he finds, rare there. Furniture found in Maryland, lined with pine is, assuredly, he thinks, from elsewhere, although he has seen one fine hunt table with a frame of white pine. I have found instances where the fronts of drawers would be of Southern pine veneered with mahogany, the back piece of Southern pine, from the period of 1790 to 1820.

Dr. Berkley calls particular attention to the virtues of the various types of tulip, or poplar, as used extensively in Maryland for framework. Planing well, and sawing without splitting, it is soft as pine, and is easily worked, growing straight and tall with a diameter of six or eight feet. He recites its freedom from knots, the fact that it does not buckle or twist when wet, and that it is seemingly not affected by the changes of time. It was used, he says, for frames and drawer lining from earliest colonial days, in Southern Maryland; and New York and Philadelphia craftsmen later employed it, as did the great Chippendale, but it has not been used—except, perhaps, in Norfolk—in the South, where yellow pine is the predominant wood for bottoms and sides of drawers.

IV

FURNITURE OF THE PIONEERS

AMERICA, in the first fifty years of her existence, was largely under control of the British influence in many ways, and the idea of house and furniture clung closely to early English tradition, when many often slept in one bed, none too comfortable, and wherever a fireplace happened to be. Chairs were unusual, the use of them attended with such ceremony as the commoner seldom attained to. The wainscot chair, the early important British chair, with its rectangular joinings, upstanding posts and heavy stretchers, thought in fact to have descended from old church chairs, and used on occasions of state in England, has been copied both in the North and South.

The first Southern settlers, in many instances, could do no better for themselves by way of shelter than huts and cabins, and even caves, with the Cavalier-born, as well as the less fortunate, having to bide their time until something better could be produced. Following the cabins in Maryland, came the pine-board house, green-shingled and shuttered or paneled at the windows, and as housebuilding got under way in Maryland and Virginia, the barn-type house, with high pitched roofs, and chimneys built outside the walls, largely prevailed. The general type in Virginia clung to the idea of the central hall with two large rooms on either side.

The use of tents has been implied for the early settlers of the Clarendon colony to the South, but some of the South Carolina colonists lived in mud and clay houses of a better type, one of which is said to have stood to this day near Kingstree, in Williamsburg County. An example of the houses built of native cement, composed of lime and oyster shell, tabby, as it is called, is that on Fripp's Island, near Beaufort. Early houses, too, were built sometimes of marl, in South Carolina.

The early artisans and laborers found their comfort in nothing short of peg-legged stools, plank tables rudely set up, and benches with pillows of pine, when they could get them for furniture; but it was not to continue so with the wealthy men of the colonies, with dignity in their living early presenting itself. Finding themselves possessed of numberless slaves and far-reaching lands, as the century progressed, they spent freely, and were, by the middle of the seventeenth century, ready to fall into line with the general movement abroad for more comfort. Their inventories and wills reveal a constant reaching out after luxuries; and some, before the century was over, were actually living in affluence and splendor.

Adam Thoroughgood, member of the King's Council, took himself a wife in 1626, and very soon built himself a house of straw-bound brick interlaid with something better, the oldest house now standing in Virginia today; and in its kitchen-dining room, in the keeping room or parlor, with paneled chimney piece and deep windows, in the hall and above the stairs, may be

15

seen something of the style of living to which even the lone planters of the day might attain.

Toddsbury, in Gloucester County, Virginia, built in 1658, a veritable gem in architectural design and execution as seen in these distant days, has remained the wonder of succeeding generations. Its maple-paneled dining room with fluted pilasters, its slow, ascending stairway, the delicacy of its balustrade and beauty of its spindles, posts and dado, help to make the wonder grow. Bacon's Castle, in Surry County, built in 1649; the Galt house in Williamsburg, where the Grand Assembly met in 1677, and others in Virginia, might be mentioned. The Wormeley house stands out, dignified, ornate, and richly furnished, where Ralph Wormeley, in the manner of a lord, lived up to the dignities of a member of the King's Council, overlooking the broad lowlands of the river.

Cross Manor, Calvert's Rest, Brushwood, on the South Wicomico, hark back to the stately days of early Maryland. The Old Brick House on the Edisto Island, in South Carolina, with its walls two feet thick, its cypress paneling and painting in oil by master hands, tells a story somewhat different from that of the oldest house at Beaufort, so arranged that muskets could be exploded from both sides, with a place provided below where ammunition might be kept at hand.

Throughout, joiners and carpenters were at work. The more prosperous depended on importation for the best of their furniture. The home craftsmen copied for the less wealthy citizens. The piece of most service was the chest, containing, as a rule,

what store of worldly goods the colonist had been allowed to bring across. "A bord of which ship I did put My Self W^th Chest and Cloathes," wrote the Reverend John Lawrence, in those early days, striking a popular note; for passage was seldom asked for without it. The finer, or "joyned" chests, came from England. The simpler chests in the South were made in cedar, spruce, oak, pine, walnut, and cypress, by which swamp pine must have been meant, is often mentioned. Carving came into the South with the later chests after the middle of the seventeenth century. Chests marked the beginning everywhere of a line of noble furniture.

Cupboards partake, throughout, of the seventeenth century forms, and were the most decorated pieces of their day, due to the various treatments they received in their design. Both the court cupboard and the press cupboard were built on the same general idea, of one carcass placed upon another. The top section of the press cupboard was similar to the lower, and closed at the bottom. That of the court cupboard was usually open, with the shelf. Cupboards of much charm of later date remain of the old South.

The earliest found in the South is the court cupboard, and the word is generally accepted as referring to the carved oak cupboard of the early seventeenth century. The earliest example presented is one which, according to design, must have been made between 1615 and 1620, and it is known to have come from Virginia. The oak Virginia-made cupboard, lined with Southern pine, which is illustrated, stamped with its early style, makes safe the assumption that this piece is one of the first made in Virginia, and as far as can be determined, the first in the United States.

Early beds in any quantity have not been found in the South. Due to their cumbersomeness, many of them have been done away with, it is thought. What the settlers made and used was simple, with the bed furniture, perhaps, of more moment than the bed. Some heavily carved oak beds may have been brought over from England in the early days, but none have survived.

The earliest tables in England had bulbous, turned legs like the turnings of the court cupboard; the large tables, with stretcher base, were in use until about 1710. The gate-leg table was generally used for a dining table and took the place of the refectory table, as it was called. A chair of the wainscot type is shown in this book, discovered in Chesterfield County, Virginia. The first quarter of the seventeenth century is the period to which this type is accredited in England. This chair, it then appears, might have been made before 1620. The Bible box, used in early days for writing, which preceded the slant-top desk of the end of this period, was the forerunner of the secretary of today.

It is to be regretted that few people in the South tried to collect these examples of furniture of this early period. Local pieces that have been found are simplified copies of English models from native woods, and the few examples that have been found, have gone to enrich private collections of the North, as pioneer dealers from other parts of America were buying the Southern-made pieces long before interest was

aroused here. Little attempt will be made here to show the influence of design on the Southern cabinetmaker prior to 1700.

With this study before us, it is not amiss to have looked into the manner of living of these pioneers, and to further acquaint ourselves with some of the types of things they used. Maryland and Virginia rooms were large, with the walls often lined, or glazed, or even figured with flowers. The colonists made much of color at the windows, on their walls and floors, and on their beds, using there such stuffs, delightfully colored, of their own devising, with finer textiles which found their way from elsewhere.

The oft quoted inventory of April 15, 1641, showed goods, as set forth by her husband, to be reserved for Dame Thoroughgood at the time of his passing. Outstanding was a bed, table, six chairs, stools, cushions, and a cupboard, all of which to make life livable for this brave lady on the waters of Lynnhaven. "Imprimis:" we read, "one bed with blankets, rug and the furniture thereto, belonging: two pairs of sheets and pillow cases; one table with carpet; table cloth and napkins, knives and forks: one cupboard and cupboard cloth two . . . one linen, one woollen, six chairs, six stools, six cushions, six pictures hanging in the chamber, one pewter basin and ewer, one warming pan, one pair andirons in the chimney, one pair tongs, one fire shovel, one chair of wicker for a child. Plate for the cupboard, one salt cellar, one bowl, one tankard, one wine cup, one dozen spoons."

William Fitzhugh, "less out for the fashions," as he said, of himself, than other

Virginia gentlemen of the late seventeenth century about him, was constrained to declare, "I neither abound nor want." He said of his house, "my own dwelling house furnished with accommodations for a comfortable and gentile living, as a good dwelling house with rooms, four of them hung, and nine of them plentifully furnished with all things necessary and convenient." But when shipping black walnut to England, however, he satisfied his longing for luxuries by ordering, by the first ship bound for his river, "a table, pair of stands, Case Drawers & looking Glass Answerable, two large leather carpets and set of dressing boxes answerable to the table and stand"; later, considerable plate, by way of knives, forks, spoons, porringers, and candlesticks, all to be crested.

Living everywhere, it would seem, had improved. A far inland mountain farmer in Rappahannock County, Virginia, George Nicholls, lists in his will, with a court cupboard, other chests and articles which even then denote decided comfort: "two tables, one six and one four foot, one form, one great looking glass, one couch, one great joyned chair, one pair of andirons . . . one feather bed and furniture, two high bedsteads."

In the records of the Society of Friends, in the Lower Meeting record books in Virginia, around 1700, is an inventory of one William Bresy, seemingly well provided for in life. Besides innumerable chairs, chests, trunks, frame cupboards, and beds, he records feather beds and furniture, one-half dozen leather chairs, three sealskin trunks, one small gilt trunk, one fine square table, one-half dozen "joyn't" stools, two "tracle" bedsteads, "three cover cloths, belonging to the cupboard in Susannah's room," three pewter "pye" plates, one pottle pot, two brass skimmers, three urn spits, two pieces of blue linen, one drip pan, two pewter chamber pots, one silver "beker," one sack cup, one silver dram cup, two old negro men, two old negro women, not to mention "one English man servant, thirty sheep, a mare and a colt."

V

STYLE DEVELOPMENT IN FURNITURE

AT THE beginning of the eighteenth century, furniture makers abandoned straight lines and turned to curves, especially in chairs. The cabriole leg was employed. After the reign of Elizabeth, turning machinery was improved, and Queen Anne herself is credited with having encouraged more decorative and graceful designs. With the Dutch influence laying the basis of the development ahead, England and France, in the first part of this half of this century, were approaching the golden period of furniture.

The first half of the century found the colonists in their living well past comfort, and many on the way to affluence and ease, the smaller men receiving their meed of good fortune as well. Governor Gooch's ruling for the inspection of tobacco in Virginia, rolled up the revenues of the plantation owners, and set more of them to building better houses and buying or making better furniture. The work of the journeymen and private craftsmen, particularly in the plantations, during these days, must not be forgotten, and such homes as these offered rich opportunity for the work there, while county records reveal, throughout the century, the journeymen at work.

Many of the better houses now were definitely elegant in structure and appointment. Early in the century, Rosewell, in Tidewater, Virginia, rose upon Carter's Creek, ponderous in style, superb in finish, with a miraculously carved stairway down which eight might walk abreast. Stratford, the home of the Lee family, in a pretentious manner, took its place above the Potomac, in 1729, in the Virginia Northern Neck. Sabine Hall, on the Rappahannock, followed the next year, marked by its elaborate joinery, cornices, pilasters and unusual stairway with twisted spindles, the painted paneling in the dining room, its library, and music room. Westover was built for the Byrds in the early thirties, in its Georgian loveliness of today, where its fading brick and fine doorway and stately entrance, formal garden, and gentle bend of the lawn to the river beneath the tulip poplars, as much as anywhere else recalls those days of stately living.

Settlement, meanwhile, had proceeded apace in the newer colonies to the south, not only on the Chowan, but at Cape Fear, where old Wilmington was showing its face; and inward, on the Cooper and Ashley, around Charles Town, the mother of the southernmost colony; on the neck of land beyond between the rivers, where the homes of the Mathews, Greens, Grays, Grimballs, and Izards might be seen with those of Land Grave Bellinger and Sir John Yeamans. Land grants along the west and east branches of the Cooper had been taken up, and homes were making on Goose Creek, and the Santees, where many Huguenots dwelt; at Georgetown, in 1734; Saint John's; Saint Mark's, including the northwest part of the State, in 1757; on the Ashley, Dorchester, and on towards Beaufort and Columbia, as time progressed.

19

The French Huguenots in South Carolina, many of them, early in the century had long since put behind them thoughts of the penury brought with them, and were reaping the reward of their thrift along with other prosperous planters. Fine, brick houses were being built around Charles Town, from 1710 until 1760, when brick and stone gave way to houses of wood on basements of brick, but with few, however, of brick in the upland county, and not many more in the central part of the State as time progressed. The three- and four-storied houses, characteristic of the place today, follow the San Domingo idea, where single rooms were built one upon the other, as if for a tower. The finer houses of the colony opened at the side, on verandahs reaching the length of the house, facing the garden, but with easy access to the street.

The city of Charles Town, visited by fire near the end of the first half of the century, with every house on the east side of Broad Street consumed, went about rebuilding herself in brick, as the period of prosperity began to make itself felt. Fine gardens were being made, with Henry Middleton at work at Middleton Place, and Mrs. Drayton at Magnolia, on the Ashley, where today, in spring, the garden still grows, and myriad of azaleas, in blossoming pink of every tint and shade, and red of every hue, mingle their tones in such fashion as to produce an almost overwhelming sense of loveliness.

Extravagance and high living was the order of the day when Governor Glenn arrived from England, in 1743. So very lavish were the colonists in spending their substance, that he was forced to declaim against it, sending word back to England of the lengths to which they went in supplying themselves with such things as silks, plate and silver and furniture out of all reason.

Drayton Hall, with its brick walls, columns of Portland marble, and wainscoting from floor to ceiling, was built in 1740, in Saint Andrew's Parish, near the Ashley River, in a section where many cultured English people made their homes. The Corbin House, at Edenton, in the province to the north, as displayed today in the Brooklyn Museum, revealing in furniture the Chippendale form, was built in 1758. Everywhere it went on, with Belair in Maryland, built in 1741, keeping the pace, showing furnishings of such value as to bring almost a thousand pounds when sold at vendue later. Fine houses and fine furniture meant fine living, and visiting back and forth, with cards and dances that lasted for days, to enjoy. Annapolis opened her theatre in 1752. Charles Town was already filling hers to the doors. Breeding of fine horses was the business and sport of a gentleman. The thoroughbred had long since displaced the field pony in Virginia, with Virginia and Maryland the pioneers in improving the stock, and many race courses being run — the York, at Charleston, highly popular, as were those at Fredericksburg and Alexandria, and on to Marlboro and Annapolis.

Cabinetmaking, too, lifted its fine head. Stylistic development had arrived. Curves in furniture, attributed to the French, was making furniture comfortable and giving it charm. New varieties of the various types were appearing, and the South was making ready to follow the fashion. Chairs of the period showed the hoop back, and the vase or the fiddle splat, and chests as well as chairs, were showing the cabriole leg. The pad foot in the South was popular with the cabriole. Chests were moving on their way, with the tall boy, of the first of the century, developing before the middle into that aristocrat of furniture, the high boy, with ogee scroll pediment; and Josiah Claypoole, as has been shown, advertising desks and bookcases, in 1740, as made in his shop with arch pediment and ogee heads.

Beds were now in the heyday of the finery of bed furniture. Back panels and tops in England were gone. Many of the Southern beds were richly carved, the majority with four tall posts, and oftener than not, a small rail or cornice around the top for holding the draperies, called a tester. Tables were showing new shape and use. The cabriole-leg table was shown with the swinging leg and two drop leaves. The three-section tables, first used in this period, were being made. Tea tables had appeared.

Desks were showing many forms, and as if to meet a growing need, the side table, or sideboard table, developing from the side table, is mentioned in the South as early as 1725, and a side, or sideboard table of walnut of a Queen Anne style, 1730-'50, is shown in this book.

In 1732 furniture making asserts itself in Charles Town definitely, through the *Gazette,* with James McClellan, from London, announcing on Church Street the making "of all sorts of Cabinet Ware, vz Cabinet desks and Bookcases, Buroes, Tables of all Sorts, Chairs, Tea Boxes and the new Fashioned Chests &c," and he was selling joiners' tools as well. Broomhead and Blythe the next year announced "Chest of Drawers, and mahogany Tables and Chairs made in the best manner," and marking, perhaps, the earliest appearance of that wood known in the South.

New men appeared then almost every year, until 1736, when we find a woman succeeding to the craft laid down by her husband, "William Watson, deceas'd, with a considerable Stock of fresh goods necessary for Funerals, and Workmen fully capable of making Coffins and Cabinet ware with Tables, Chests-of-Drawers and Buroes." Cradles this year, too, might have been bought of Charles Warham, and "a fine Easy Chair cover'd with green Silk, also a Couch with Squab cover'd the same Way," just imported, 1738, from Watson and Mackenzie.

VI

CHIPPENDALE AND REVOLUTION

AMONG the pieces for which George Washington wrote, when forwarding his well-known order for furniture to London in 1755, two years before his marriage, were "a Mahogany bedstead with carved and fluted pillars and yellow silk and worsted damask hangings; window curtains to match; six mahogany chairs with gothic arched backs and seats of yellow silk and worsted damask, an elbow chair, a fine, neat mahogany serpentine dressing table with mirrors and brass trimmings, and a pair of fine carved and gilt scones." His order was well placed and well timed. Thomas Chippendale was then at work in London.

Furniture making was now reaching the highest point of its greatness. Chippendale, working in London since 1740, had wrought a transformation. Taking what he found, he was making over all ideas of furniture and breathing into his models strength, grace, and elaboration, producing a type satisfactory, and beautiful in proportion, which was to give his name to the period from about 1750 to 1780. In 1754 he had published *The Gentleman and Cabinet Maker's Director,* to follow with later editions in 1759 and 1762, which extended his influence widely, not only at home, but in the American colonies as well.

Chippendale did not stand head and shoulders above his contemporaries, but his plates were the best in their class, and his greatness was due to the cleverness of his adaptation and the refinement of borrowed designs. Deriving richly from other in-

fluences already at work, he took what he found, and made it better, without neglecting the Dutch influence, so basic in English furniture at the time. He adopted the Gothic and Chinese motifs with striking effect, intermingling the two when occasion arose. He used oriental motifs often expressing a real meaning, as evidenced in the pagoda, the lattice and the trellis, to which he frequently resorted. He related himself, too, at times, to the Greek and Roman, as well as the French. His work is particularly remarked for his use of the cabriole leg, the introduction of which, however, is not to be credited to him, introduced as it was, into England by the Dutch, though lightened by the French and made sturdier by the English before reaching its most beautiful expression in the Chippendale shape.

The Chippendale period is sometimes designated by the claw-and-ball foot. This foot was shown first in Jacques Androuet's *Book of Designs,* published in France, 1550, the leg and claw-and-ball foot illustrated by him showing the acanthus leaf carving at the top. This, too, was a type borrowed from the Chinese design representing the serpent's claw holding a pearl. Chippendale used carving profusely, and worked constantly in mahogany, and produced marvels in his veneered surfaces of this satiny wood. Mahogany came into use as the most popular wood during this period in England, although it was used as early as 1710.

His furniture, fitting well into the scheme.

of living of the more wealthy British, and much of its splendor highly in keeping with the sumptuousness with which British nobility surrounded itself, was however, far too ornate for general practical purpose, and transitions of his designs were widely effected for those wishing something less elaborate. London cabinet-makers of his day were constantly at work on simpler interpretations of his designs, and the type that came to America was of this class. Pieces of Southern-made furniture found, after the Chippendale manner, while not as sophisticated as the English examples, have a great deal of charm.

Chippendale was distinctly felt below the Potomac, and his influence shows generally in the types extant today; cupboards, side tables, tables, cellarets, and chairs of course, fell under the dominance of his interest. With so much around them by way of example, men from London easily in touch with it, arriving constantly among them, the Southern craftsmen could do no other than to aspire to its beauty.

Much is to be said of the Chippendale chair: the influence of the Dutch in the understructure; the Queen Anne vase design, and the piercing of the splat; the ladder backs, the ribbands; fret work and interlaced effects; the intermingling of types; the oriental trellis and pagoda; the Gothic motifs; some of the chairs with square legs and understretchers, and some with cabriole and drop seat widening toward the front; the fine, top rail and its upward curving—all serve to make it what it is.

Among the chairs presented for examination, it has been made possible to show examples from 1760-1780 of the major types of the backs he employed. There is a fine old walnut armchair, showing the derivation of the fiddle-back; a Southern chair in mahogany, approaching in manner the ribband-back chair, although varied with a scroll and so faithful in detail as to appear almost a reproduction; a ladder-back, of mahogany, with sunk or hollowed seat, and a Chippendale side and corner chair, from an old mansion house in middle Virginia, reflecting the ideas of the great draftsman and designer, whose pencil, as he said, but faintly copied those images that his fancy suggested.

Tables of the period, in various designs, likewise reflected the Chippendale idea. This is evidenced in side tables in a variety of examples, and in three-section dining tables which were likewise employed.

A Chippendale table, showing the claw-and-ball foot will be later exemplified. There is a Chippendale walnut mixing table, 1760-1770, and the majority of cellarets show the Chippendale influence, and that of Hepplewhite, following after. This was the period of the pie-crust table; the first with raised rim, and the Pembroke table also appeared at this time.

The influence of Chippendale on the Southern cupboard reveals itself to fine effect in two different types. The side tables, too, show Chippendale designs, with one discovered particularly well worked out in fine detail. The Moravians made their appearance at Salem at the turn of the second half of the century, and the same Chippendale influence is felt in the furniture of the churchmen, furniture lovers finding much thrilling to them in a corner cupboard of individual execution, following in construction the English master.

South Carolina, at that time, was fully awake, it would seem, as to what was going on in furniture across the water: Thomas Lining, 1754, from London, selling all sorts of cabinet and chair work "well finished and in the most fashionable manner"; Peter Hall, also from London, holding forth on the Bay, "where Gentlemen and Ladies of taste may have made, and be supplied with Chinese Tables of all Sorts, Shelves, Trays, Chimney Pieces, Brackets, being at present the most elegant and admired in London." Solomon Legeré made chairs at the plantation on John's Island; John Biggard, 1767, from Philadelphia, had a turner's shop on the Bay at Queen Street, where Windsor and garden chairs might be supplied. How and Roulain, 1762, Joshua Eden, in 1767, making column bedposts, table frames and straw-bottom chairs, and John Fisher, the same year, were all at work.

Thomas Elfe, from whom Washington might have bought his curtains, had long since announced, through the *Gazette,* 1751, "a very good upholsterer from London," stating that he did "all sorts of upholsterer's work, viz., tapestry, damask, stuff, chintz or paper hangings for rooms, beds after the newest fashion, and so that they may be taken off to be washed without inconvenience or damage; all sorts of festoons and window curtains to draw up, and pull rod curtains; chairs stuff-covered, tight or loose cases for ditto; all kinds of Machine Chairs are likewise made, stuff'd and cover'd for sickly or weak people."

Business in the '60's flourished on Mary-

land soil; and in the early furniture of the day, the names of Moore and the Andersons must be called. Gerrard Hopkins, in Baltimore, 1767, was selling "the newest fashions in mahogany, walnut and cherry, tea chests, desks, bookcases, scrutoires, clothes presses, tables, bureaus, card, parlour and tea tables, chairs, candle stands, decanter stands, tea kettle stands, dumb waiters, tea boards, corner chairs, bedsteads, etc. etc., with or without carved work."

South Carolina colonists had not remained untouched by colonial reaction against the Stamp Act and tax importation injustices, but the English influence continued to be felt as the Revolution approached, and luxuries remained almost to the end. In 1771 Richard Magrath, fine copyist of Manigault importations, who, "having labored under a bad state of health," announced in the *Gazette* that he "intends to remove up the path a little way out of the Town gate," where there would be "much to sell by way of carved chairs, with Commode fronts and Pincushion Seats of the newest fashion and the first of that Construction ever made in this Province," close stools, elbow chairs likewise listed; but two years later, as the war approached, he was offering, "by Publick Sale, . . . Sophas, French Chairs, Conversation Stools and Easy Chairs of the newest fashion and neatest Construction, such as were never offered for sale in this Province before . . . the greatest Sale of neat Cabinet Work ever known in this Place."

John Dobbins, we read in 1770, "departing the Province in the Spring, was selling by public vendue . . . Chinese Tables, carved and plain, mahogany bedsteads, neat double and half chests of drawers; French Chairs, brass nailed ditto," adding that "Three month's credit will be given for all sums above twenty pounds."

Everywhere, elegance and ease and the quest for the beautiful was in order, with Charles Town, the year 1765, graced by the Miles Brewton House, at High Street, in all its basemented splendor and French curving entrance and balustrade, its wide, flagged hall having a broad mahogany stairway, its cornices and chimney pieces and its doorway with exquisitely carved frame and forelight. Here may be seen the work of Waite, the English architect and carver from London who, according to his own statement, had had experience "both in theory and practice in noblemen's and gentlemen's seats," and who planned and "carved all the said work in the four principal rooms, and also calculated, adjusted, and draw'd at large for to work by the Ionick entablature, and carved the same in front and round the eaves." This house is known today as the Pringle House. The Horry House came in 1767.

There was elegance among the planters, and leisure, if desired, on from the middle of the century, with building activity continued, as the struggles with the French and Indians ended. Carter's Grove, in Virginia, built in 1751, showed doorways flanked with pilasters, hand-tooled work in the drawing room, fronting the river,

a Roman Doric cornice above its chimney piece, and easy-falling stairway with twisted newels and fine ramp, an archway eighteen feet wide, flanked by Ionic pilasters breaking the wall paneled in black walnut and pine. Kenmore, in Fredericksburg on the Rappahannock, where Betty Washington Lewis made her home, with her mother hard by, was a house of stately proportion; but at Gunston Hall, trim and all neat, above the Potomac, 1755, to which spot he had brought his fifteen-year-old Maryland bride, George Mason sat and pondered on the rights of man. Trouble was brewing. So, with the war upon him, Thomas Jefferson, at Monticello, in the early '70's was soon to halt his task. He was then engaged with the classical revival of architecture and preparing to strike the note of white-columned beauty in the mansion he was building there, to be taken up by many Southern mansions elsewhere, and carried to its highest peak of excellence in the State capitol and University.

Washington, at Mount Vernon, in 1774, as the grievance increased, sent no more to England, but satisfied himself with luxuries bought much nearer home when the Fairfax furniture was sold at Belvoir, taking in a mahogany shaving set, a settee bed and furniture, the mahogany chest and drawers that had stood in Mrs. Fairfax's chamber, one mahogany sideboard, twelve chairs, one mahogany desk, and one mahogany close stool.

VII

CLASSICISM AND THE REPUBLIC

BUT a change in furniture making was ahead, with the influence of Chippendale interrupted and a reaction against the elaborateness of his design setting in. A new note was being sounded, a new idea infusing itself, which meant a breaking away from the rococo, and a turning to classic lines in furniture, as in architecture. The chief exponent of this revival was Robert Adam, one of three brothers working to that end, from 1750 to 1794, at London.

In southern Europe, Adam had been stirred by the remains of classic architecture, and having been thrown there with a group engaged in excavation and study of the ruins below Vesuvius, and particularly inspired by what he saw of the remains of Pompeii, he came back to England to set in motion waves of influence in architecture and furniture felt distinctly in the United States. He was an architect—in fact, architect to the king, after his return to London. He made no furniture, but in planning his houses, he designed furniture entirely in keeping with them, in plan and detail.

His general schemes followed architectural lines and form. He was consistent in the use of scale, and absolutely sensitive to size relation of all elements involved. He made much change in detail, and used many decorations, much of which was done by the best artists of the day. The Adam brothers collaborated with Angelica Kaufman, Pergolessi, Zucchi, and others, and their designs were full of elegance, made up of classical motifs. The three brothers published thirty volumes of designs for architects, and although the Revolutionary War interrupted their influence, it was extended later when Hepplewhite came into vogue.

Hepplewhite's ideas of furniture building came to America following the Revolution, as the country, too, responded at length to the Adam idea. The period of his activity corresponded largely, in time, to that of the administration of George Washington as President of the United States, when the country was again making some advance, and the ideas of luxurious living once more were uppermost. The Hepplewhite name designates a furniture rapidly coming into favor as the new republic got upon its feet.

The Cabinet Makers' London Book of Prices, by Shearer and Hepplewhite, was published in 1788, in England, by Thomas Shearer, a man whose work in furniture is almost unknown in America, but Hepplewhite's name designates a style in furniture popular here. *The Cabinet Makers' and Upholsterer's Guide and Repository of Designs for Every Article of Household Furniture,* in three editions, appearing successively in 1788-'89-'90, brought out by his wife after his death, served of course, to make him better known. His earliest pieces and his books gained him a wide circle of followers.

The years of influence credited to him

extended only from about 1788-1795, but Southern workmen were influenced by the Hepplewhite style as late as 1815, and the bulk of Southern-made furniture is of Hepplewhite style, with the trend of design continuously toward the lighter and more decorative pieces. Much of the influence of Adam is seen in that of Hepplewhite; his designs, as published, often a transition from Adam to the more practical, the Hepplewhite design making a transition from the more refined and delicate classic to something more practical, and easily followed. Hepplewhite, disregarding the Chippendale tradition of design, used the subtle curve, and decorated his furniture, which was oftenest of light wood, with inlay and painting rather than with so much carving, which, it is true, he used often when working in mahogany.

Hundreds of cabinetmakers worked at London, and in 1790 there appeared among them a strange figure, to remain for sixteen years. This was Thomas Sheraton, a man without means, living on a poor street, wearing a worn and threadbare coat, and combining with his piety, as a minister of the Gospel, a genius for conception of beautiful furniture that perhaps has never been excelled. He registered as an author, bookseller, scholar, and preacher. His ideas of design were built largely around those of the Adam brothers, and he was ready to carry forward the classical idea, so much like Adam and at times so like Hepplewhite, that it is difficult to distinguish him from them. But in his designing he improved what he took so freely and made lighter and more decorative pieces, always with an artistic feeling of line and propor-

tion. In 1791 he published *The Cabinet Makers and Upholsterer's Drawing Book.*

In 1804 he published the *Cabinet Makers' and General Artists' Encyclopedia,* containing thirty parts, further projecting his ideas of grace in design, and delicacy and refinement in decoration, so that in America, where books were published in imitation of those the master designers had brought out, his name became a household word. Strong influence of the Roman, Tuscan, and Greek was shown in the book. His appeal was to the practical as well as the fastidious, and the charming quality of what he had to offer, was highly satisfactory in its delicacy, strength, and beauty.

Southern craftsmen seized upon his designs, and his motifs, combined with those of Hepplewhite, are reflected widely in their work in their native woods. His influence here meant lighter forms of furniture, and his use of inlaid motifs for decoration became highly popular in this country; light-colored woods, and the use of apple, tulip, satinwood, mahogany and rosewood veneer is remarked. Sheraton pieces, found in the South, depend largely on inlay for ornamentation.

Duncan Phyfe, outstanding American cabinetmaker of New York, employed perhaps one hundred men, and his influence undoubtedly spread throughout the South. Phyfe showed a distinct classic influence, and followed Hepplewhite and Sheraton, with French leanings at times, 1795-1820, until the Empire period reached America. His works came South and were copied by Southerners, and perhaps even by men who had been employed in his own shops. Among others influencing workmen who came South, or who copied their pieces brought there, were Randolph, Savery, and Gostelowe, of Philadelphia, all men of eminence.

The sideboards of Hepplewhite, with the serpentine front, so delighted the heart of the Southern workmen that numerous examples have been found. Sheraton sideboards, showing the round ends, the straight or concave center and turned or reeded legs, are reproduced in much simpler fashion than those designed by the master, but examples have been found of various woods and inlay and veneer that he employed.

Beautiful examples of Hepplewhite beds have been found, reflecting much practice and skill on the part of the craftsman at work. Excellent examples of Hepplewhite and Sheraton beds have been seen in South Carolina, sawed up in such a way as to be used for tables; and one pair of elaborate posts was found painted and doing duty as supports for an otherwise failing porch in Wake County, North Carolina.

The Hepplewhite chair is easily distinguished by the Hepplewhite shield, and is often used in delicate poise in American chairs, although the heart shape, which he likewise used, is often introduced. The Sheraton influence in chairs is abundant, although it is difficult to find examples of first quality, beautifully proportioned and classic in line as they were. The square leg, with arrow-motif back is shown, the square, tapered leg, showing in the South, in many types. The distinguishing mark of his chairs were the straight lines employed, where Hepplewhite delighted in curves. Whether the top rail was curved or straight,

Sheraton lifted up the splat and, putting in a connecting slat between the posts, provided a square frame for ornamenting the center as he might desire. Fine textiles were employed for his chair seats, adding immeasurably to their beauty.

Chests, chests of drawers, and cupboards through the South reflect the Hepplewhite influence; cellarets, too, show the inspiration of this master. Many examples of movable corner cupboards in mahogany are found, some of them showing the familiar inlay and tracing of design in wood, as in his chairs. Tambour desks were popular under the influence of both Hepplewhite and Sheraton, and Southern workmen left much behind them that showed ingenuity of craftsmanship in working out their designs.

*   *   *   *

With Washington in the presidency, a new note of confidence was sounded, to which, in some cases, the South was slow to respond, due to its ravished condition and the distress occasioned by the inability of the people to collect on government loans made during the war. The bad situation, however, began slowly to mend with the inadequacies of the early federal government, particularly in finance, superseded by something more stable in 1790. Order began to appear out of chaos, and conditions in the South gradually improved.

In rough figures, there were now nearly two million people in the South, and many of the middle class and lesser planters needed more and more furniture, and they needed it badly; but there were other things that they needed more, with prosperity slow in smiling upon them. The wealthy, however, recovered themselves, and importations were again indulged in despite the bitter memories of the war, and the South's active protests against the overweening British influence in the North, and, as Jeffersonians claimed, on the government itself.

Washington's administration had been set up with style, and an amazing degree of elegance and fine living, likewise, among the wealthy in the South, was renewed. New life was apparent through the United States, as the new century dawned upon them. Cities grew, and money became more abundant in the South.

There is slight evidence of any furniture making in Baltimore during the early bitterness of the Revolution, and certainly not until after 1780, when Mr. Chisholm, we are told, took up the task. John Lindsay, just out of London, shortly arrived at Dumfries; and in Charleston, from the story the newspapers have to tell, business seemed largely stagnant. The Baltimore business, however, seemed to have picked up, following 1780, with a steady list of craftsmen there busy as well. Following 1800, when the federal government was removed from Philadelphia to the new Federal City on the Potomac, Baltimore became a shopping center for furniture.

Charleston furniture makers were more slow to recover themselves from the effect of the war, but the need of some of them to make coffins and supply funeral necessities, as had been their custom from early times, made them a necessary adjunct to business, whatever else their condition might have been. The year after Sheraton appeared in London, 1791, in the period

generally ascribed to Hepplewhite, we find as announced by the *Gazette,* that Andrew Gifford, "Just from New York has for sale Mahogany Furniture, Desks, Bookcases, Secretary, Oval Tables, Inlaid Table, Card Table, sideboards, plain and inlaid, Dining Tables in Setts, Pembroke Tables in Setts, Circular Tables, Night Tables, Settees, Sofas, Chairs of best Pattern, an Elegant Clock and Case, Bedsteads, Chest of Drawers, Single Tables in Setts, Bason Stands."

In December, 1790, we find Solomon Smith informing his friends "That he has returned to the Province," and is carrying on the "Upholsterer's Business," selling, at No. 8 Tradd Street, camp beds, and bedsteads with springs and cases, lookingglasses, inlaid tea tables and trays; Wallace and Watts, "Cabinet and Piano Forte makers from London," were carrying on in Meeting Street.

It was at the turn of the century that the business in Charleston began to speak for itself again through the newspapers, directories, and other agencies in any compelling number. Once it was started, there was such a flood of men at work, men of various extraction, as the following list will indicate: Coquereau, Muckenfus, Naser, Horlbeck, Peigne, Rou, Row, Sass, Sigwald, Tamerus, Tennant, Quackenbush, Marlen, Mellichamp, Mellise and hosts of others, whose varied birth undoubtedly influenced the undertaking in which they were engaged, particularly those of French and West Indian extraction.

Richmond came into its own early in the eighties, when the capital was removed there from Williamsburg. Life quickened, particularly following the close of the war. Furniture making discloses itself to us there, as always in Virginia, not as an established business, but the result of private labor. Extended notice of work carried on in Richmond is revealed, and there are names at this time that may be called. The names of Andrew and Robert Mc-Kimm appear on one of the labels given in this book, and the name of Robert is listed in the first census of Richmond, as is that of William Pointer, listed in the census of 1782. In 1807 John Alcock advertised in the *Enquirer,* of Richmond, and again in 1809, informing the public that he was "carrying on his Cabinet Makers' Business in all its branches where he makes all kinds of Mahogany Furniture in the best manner."

*   *   *   *

The Empire influence in furniture set in about 1820; and the reign of beauty was over. Much of the best that had been accomplished by way of lightening and giving grace and proportion to furniture was forced out, to make way for the more imposing pieces, impressive mainly on account of their size and heavy carving. Some of the workmanship was exceedingly good, as many of the best masters worked at it everywhere, as the vogue for what was French followed the rise of Napoleon's fortunes.

The spiral twist came in as motif during this period, and was found on legs of furniture and used often on bedposts. Headboards, as a rule, became more elaborate, and with the rooms in Southern houses large, it is not surprising that many of the Empire beds are to be found in the South. The pineapple motif, signifying plenty, was used to such an extent that the Empire period in the South has been often referred to as the Pineapple period.

VIII

SEEKING SOUTHERN ANTIQUES

INTO this land filled with the memory of high achievement, distinction in living, beauty and refinement in concept and execution, I have gone on a search a bit late; for much of the furniture imported or local-made has long since been deported by pioneer collectors before the South awoke to the value of what it possessed. But I have gone in time to find enough to tell the fine story of the pioneer workers in furniture in the South, and bring abundant example of the development of a craft long since gone. I have gone through almost trackless forests, over rugged roads, to crumbling doorways; I have gone on the spur of the moment of notice of a sale or of any division of an estate, the breaking up of a home, or the division of property.

It is not always that I have gone to some white-columned mansion of other days and lifted a knocker at gleaming portals, where within its guarded confines rare pieces were well preserved. The doorways at which entrance has often been sought, have been largely neglected doors, along the river country where old settlements remain to tell the story of grandeur now departed. Forgotten doors, they sometimes were, even to columned houses, fallen from their high estate, passed into disuse and decay, and sometimes even into the hands of negroes. Some of the furniture, its value unrecognized, its owners having yielded to indifference or necessity has been burnt at the woodpile for kindling, as being in the way, shoved off on some poor relative or servant, or taken up at vendues or sales by the negroes of the neighborhood. Some of it is still to be found within.

The whole State of Virginia has furnished a rich mine of treasure. From the coast inward, up the bay, and along the Potomac, the James, the York, and the Rappahannock Rivers, and at Jamestown and Yorktown, rich fields are offered for study and research. At Alexandria and at Fredericksburg, where cabinetmaking was done, and many fine inlaid pieces have been found, the supply is seemingly exhausted. Portsmouth and Suffolk offer a particularly fine opportunity for the collector, and the yield is good in Norfolk, Williamsburg, and in Richmond. In Charlottesville, and Albemarle County, where home-making was at its best, and the refining influence of Thomas Jefferson was felt, real results have been obtained, with fine, inlaid pieces likewise found there. Wheeling (now in West Virginia) cultivated the craft, and offers opportunity. In the Shenandoah Valley, and along what was once the post road, established in 1782, reaching down into North Carolina, many relics of the furniture of the past are found.

Maryland antiques are more difficult to discover, except the highly valued pieces, although there is an effort there, as elsewhere, to bring back into the State the finer original pieces which have disappeared; but about the shores of its many rivers, however, numerous examples of the skilled workers who strove so well in Annapolis and Baltimore, are constantly being unearthed.

Berkley attributes the fact that so few pieces there have actually survived to the Law of Vendue, which required an auction sale of all effects when there was no will for probate, and recites the same story of the path to destruction that much of value in Maryland, as elsewhere, has trod from the attic to the woodpile for kindling.

North Carolina, presenting some of the best examples, is an unusually rich section, particularly in the western part of the State. Mecklenburg County is outstanding, and in the sections around Edenton, Bath, Hillsboro, New Bern, and Pittsboro, pieces of excellence have been discovered, including examples of merit of the style of the last quarter of the eighteenth century. In the vicinity of Raleigh, Greensboro, and Edenton, many fine, inlaid pieces are found of Hepplewhite and Sheraton style. From North Carolina comes the majority of the Hepplewhite tambour desks. Furniture made by the Moravians is not always definite as to the exact location in which it was discovered.

The English influence is particularly remarked in and around Savannah, and importations there and throughout the State were largely the rule. Many New England pieces are found in Georgia, obviously transported there through Savannah. New York, Boston, and Philadelphia cabinet shops had branches or warehouses in Charleston and Savannah.

On the other hand, as productive as any other Southern territory, is that of South Carolina, a rich mine of treasure within itself, and more particularly abundant along the banks of the Broad River, and around Charleston, where so much furniture activity existed, with shops on King Street, Queen Street, Meeting, the Bay, and elsewhere. Fairfields County, with its ghostlike houses in their decrepitude, sentineled by decaying columns, seemingly reminiscent of an outraged past, sets the heart of the collector a-flutter. These houses are found in the saddest of condition, a Sheraton bed, discovered in one of them, having been sawed into pieces and made into a bench.

Every collector carries with him the memory of his first big find; and it was in these sunny fields that I made my first incursion into the realm of furniture seeking. The first trip with which this book is concerned, found the writer there projected on his way with money in hand, in quest of a sideboard. I was buying the sideboard for my father who, aside from having a picture of what he wanted, had little information concerning it to offer me. With a small boy as guide, I set out, and found a sideboard at the place designated by a friend; the owner of it a woman, was in doubt as to whether she wanted to sell, but she gave me a clue to another, the owner of which was anxious to bargain at fifty dollars. To this I agreed, but she must throw in an old clock case which my eye had discovered among her possessions. She would, and I left her the money, agreeing to come back later for my purchase. The week following, I went down and secured them, forwarding my father his sideboard and bought another at reasonable price, to which the lady of the moment also held title, proposing to start my own private collection. Then yielding to the memory of the first of the three sideboards I had encountered, which still lingered with me, I sought out the lady in possession, who was now ready to sell. One hundred dollars was the amount asked. This, too, was seized upon. Whereupon, I sold the second and took the proceeds to have the third repaired, providing myself with a piece small money will not buy.

Accent, or manner foreign to the locality, is against the buyer. Various strategies must be employed. The question of values is always a delicate one, and even though well-to-do people of established financial and social position are hard to bargain with, the experienced collector always prefers to deal with someone having some idea of value and a definite figure in mind. For the day is long gone when the buyer is out to deceive the owner as to proper values, even though, as yet, the average buyer is not adverse to making a good bargain.

Ready money, flaunted in the face of the owner, seventy-five new paper dollars, as in one instance, brought prompt results with me. Some hedging, and even side-stepping a bit, is often in order on both sides, which, when it comes to the naming of price, often operates to the grief of one or the other in reality wishing to sell or buy. Ten dollars, on one occasion, offered as a start, for a tambour desk by a buyer who, in fact, would have gladly given two hundred dollars to possess it, threw the owner, a woman, into a state of indignation. "Not a penny less than twenty dol-

lars," was her answer, and the bargain was concluded on that basis.

Dealers, often too, lose out. A fair price, offered by a collector, while rambling around in a South Carolina attic with a family group who, at his suggestion, had unearthed a complete set of dining room furniture of distinct value, but long since discarded for a more modern set, led to their refusal for anything except an extortionate price—so possessed had they become with the fictitious idea of its value, and the possibility of demanding a highly inflated price. This led to the set being returned to its former setting and the collector reflecting on a lost opportunity, because he had offered something reasonable in the beginning.

Those that are anxious to sell, sometimes exhibit, unexpectedly, so much enthusiasm, that it is not always difficult to read what is actually in their minds. Stories are kept on hand in limitless numbers, particularly in the rural sections, and are shot at the unsuspecting buyer in such a way as to make him a bit wary when it comes to the actual transaction. Something that has to do with the War Between the States is the first preference, with General Sherman running as a general favorite, and given credit for having had to do with more tables, sat in more chairs, looked under more beds, and eaten from more sideboards than the capacity of any man would allow; but even these do not always bring success. Held liable for one hole in a slant-top desk, the General was represented as having gotten into the desk by another, but this did not work. The buyer was sure that even Sherman himself, diligent as he was in small things, could not have put himself through, and so assured the seller. Even the disaster of a tureen top knocked off, and charged up to Sherman, who unknowingly, it seemed, had stopped off in his march to the sea to commit the blunder, failed to make the sale.

The buyer, furthermore, is not above appealing to the emotions, and this, in certain cases, has been known to bring results. Two buyers in Raleigh, North Carolina, moved by a gate-leg table in a negro cabin in the country, to the amount of one hundred real gold dollars spread out before the owner, were amazed to find him deciding that he did not want to sell, and those around him asking him if for any reason he had suddenly "gone crazy."

IX

SIDEBOARDS

SIDEBOARDS have had to make no bid for popularity. The curve of the serpentine and bow (the Southern serpentine is flatter than those found in the North), the concave and the convex, the fine-grained walnut, soft finished mahogany, brought from the West Indies, native cherry in feathery grain, with inlaid ebony and tulip, fine bandings of kingwood, all reflecting in detail, as in other Southern-made pieces, the harmony and inspiration of the English masters by men at work at the bench.

Sideboards arose to meet a distinct need; and in that land of plenty below George Washington's "Patomack," they have done a noble part. Once in use, they served, not only to store the wines and silver and catch, as they often did in their fine surfaces, candlelight as reflected in crested silver with which they were adorned, but when eating was in process, to act as a serving table from which food in great variety was dispensed with prodigality.

The progress of the sideboard was an orderly one. Old chests served for duty, perhaps, along with the first rude tables that were set up out of old plank boards. Old cupboards, too, offered their ample shelves to help supply the need; but when they were discarded in favor of the corner cupboard, side tables, as referred to in early inventories, came in—side tables being mentioned as early as 1725, it is recalled. Some of these tables frequently had marble tops. A large Chippendale-style table, with some carving, is shown, but no advance toward the sideboard was made in the South or elsewhere during that period. Robert Adam it was who employed side tables with pedestals, one at each end, surmounted each with an urn, one used for hot and the other for cold water, the two later to become knife boxes.

In 1788 Thomas Shearer published his unique design, showing a compact piece; and the sideboard had arrived. Hepplewhite turned his attention to it, and gave it much variety. His ideas, as well as those of Sheraton, who likewise took up the theme, were popular in great measure in the South. Following Chippendale, and into the Empire period, mahogany had

Inlay found on a sideboard made in North Carolina

been the popular wood for all pieces, and the finer sideboards were made of mahogany and elaborately inlaid. Walnut was used for other boards; and so many simple inlaid walnut sideboards have been found that one can hardly imagine a Southern home without one, unless something better could be afforded.

The distinguishing characteristic of the Hepplewhite and Sheraton sideboards have been well pointed out as consisting of a difference in style of the corners employed, and the treatment of the legs of the piece. Hepplewhite produced the serpentine effect by making his corners concave. Sheraton used the convex. Hepplewhite tapered the legs of his sideboard. Sheraton reeded his, but also used the square, tapered leg. Thomas Jefferson has left a record of an "elegant sideboard with pedestals" in his private dining room at Washington, used along with the black and gold chairs, the girandole mirror and screens that helped to make up the furniture of the room, which is of interest in this connection, with Sheraton-style sideboards distinguished by the round ends and straight or concave centers.

His designs were for utility, and one of his boards carried a grate at one end for holding coals to keep the dishes warm. His turned or reeded legs were typical of the Sheraton style as interpreted by Southern workmen. Both periods, in fact, were reflected in their work, and straight and bow-front inlaid sideboards are found made as late as 1810. At this time the columns showing the Empire influence appeared at the front of sideboards, which grew steadily heavier during this period.

PLATES

PLATE I. QUEEN ANNE SIDE OR SIDEBOARD TABLE—WALNUT. (Virginia—c. 1730-1750). This type, about five feet long and from six to twelve inches taller than the average table, is the forerunner of the sideboard, and is often mentioned in inventories as a sideboard. The cabriole leg and pad foot, as shown, are typical of the period. Side and sideboard tables are found with the skirt cut in scrolls by way of ornamentation, and marble tops as much as six feet in length adorned them. Some had drawers in the front. (Property of Ross E. Millhiser).

PLATE II. CHIPPENDALE SIDE OR SIDEBOARD TABLE—WALNUT. (North Carolina—c. 1760-1770). This type, in design, is almost an exact copy of one of the Chippendale plates, showing the square leg with thumb-print grooving and cut-out corner brackets. Due to its large size, it could be used as a sideboard. Tables of this type are found embellished with carving. (Property of J. F. Geisinger).

PLATE III. HEPPLEWHITE SERPENTINE FRONT SIDEBOARD—WALNUT. (North Carolina—c. 1790). This sideboard, showing a serpentine front, is in a style which is invariably accompanied by a wine drawer at one end. The drawer fronts show a veneer of curly walnut inlaid with tulipwood and cross-banded with mahogany. The piece reflects the work of a skilled Southern craftsman. (Property of Mrs. M. A. Robbins).

PLATE IV. HEPPLEWHITE SERPENTINE SIDEBOARD—MAHOGANY. (North Carolina—c. 1790). Connoisseurs consider this to be the finest type sideboard. It is of superlative workmanship, of choice wood, and the inlaid satinwood panels in the legs add distinction. It is one of the finest pieces the author has examined. (Property of W. S. Ahern).

PLATE V. TOP—HEPPLEWHITE SERPENTINE SIDEBOARD—MAHOGANY. (South Carolina—c. 1790). This piece follows the shape illustrated in Plate IV, and shows the oval line inlay. The edge of the top has the round moulded veneer often found on Southern sideboards. (Property of Mrs. R. G. Cabell).

PLATE V. BOTTOM — HEPPLEWHITE SIDEBOARD — MAHOGANY. (South Carolina—c. 1790-1800). A sideboard having a bow center and concave ends; in reality a serpentine shape but not in a continuous curve. This type, with the additional raised top, is often found, but rarely with the concave ends. (Property of Mrs. Paul Chatham).

PLATE VI. HEPPLEWHITE HALF-ROUND SIDEBOARD — MAHOGANY. (North Carolina—c. 1790). This type of sideboard, showing the bellflower in simple inlay in the leg, is one of excellent workmanship, and no other of this type has been seen by the author in the South, but two others are said to exist. This type of inlay is often found on the legs of Southern sideboards. (Property of Mrs. M. A. Devereaux).

PLATE VII. SHERATON SIDEBOARD— MAHOGANY. (Virginia—c. 1795-1800). This Sheraton sideboard shows a concave center, the concave said to have made the entire surface of the board more easy of access, with the upright wine drawers taking a separate place, partitioned off for bottles. The square, tapered leg changes only in rare instances up to the close of 1700. The small drawers are for cutlery. Fine triple inlay is seen on the door and drawer fronts. The knife boxes are from Baltimore. The majority of knife boxes found are of English origin, and there is doubt as to whether knife boxes in any quantity were made in the Southern colonies at all. (Property of J. Pope Nash).

PLATE VIII. SHERATON BOW-CENTER SIDEBOARD—MAHOGANY AND CHERRY. (South Carolina—c. 1800). Native cherry is used to advantage in this Sheraton bow-center sideboard showing a veneer of light, feathery grain with inlaid ebony and tulipwood. The front legs and bands are mahogany, the top, sides and back legs are red cherry. These sideboards, discovered in South Carolina, may be attributed to some unknown workmanship in one of the Carolinas; for many sideboards with this bow in the center are found throughout these two states. (Property of J. R. Burroughs).

PLATE IX. SHERATON-SHAPED FRONT SIDEBOARD—WALNUT. (Georgia—c. 1795-1800). This sideboard resembles the design of the Brothers Adam and was used by Sheraton; and it is reasonable to suppose that it was made in the later period. Finely grained native walnut is used as veneer, and four such pieces of this type have been found. Though odd in shape, are all of excellent workmanship. (Property of C. G. Wyatt).

PLATE X. SHERATON STRAIGHT FRONT SIDEBOARD—CHERRY. (South Carolina—c. 1800). This sideboard of the straight front type was found near Greenville. Straight front sideboards made by the better workmen often show elaborate inlay rather than curves. Here a different placement of the wine drawers is shown. The narrow wine drawer did not come into use until the Sheraton period, and it is thought that they are of American origin. (Property of J. D. Holt).

PLATE XI. TOP—SHERATON SIDEBOARD—MAHOGANY. (Virginia—c. 1800-1820). A bow-center sideboard of the late Sheraton style, and a finely veneered piece of its type. Sideboards of this shape are found throughout the South. (Property of Mrs. Victor Stewart).

PLATE XI. BOTTOM—EMPIRE SIDEBOARD—MAHOGANY. (South Carolina—c. 1820). The ornate Empire style is shown with the crotch mahogany veneers and brass trimmings typical of this period. Although this sideboard cannot definitely be placed as Southern made, it represents a type that was made here. In the Pringle house, Charleston. (Property of Miss Susan B. Frost).

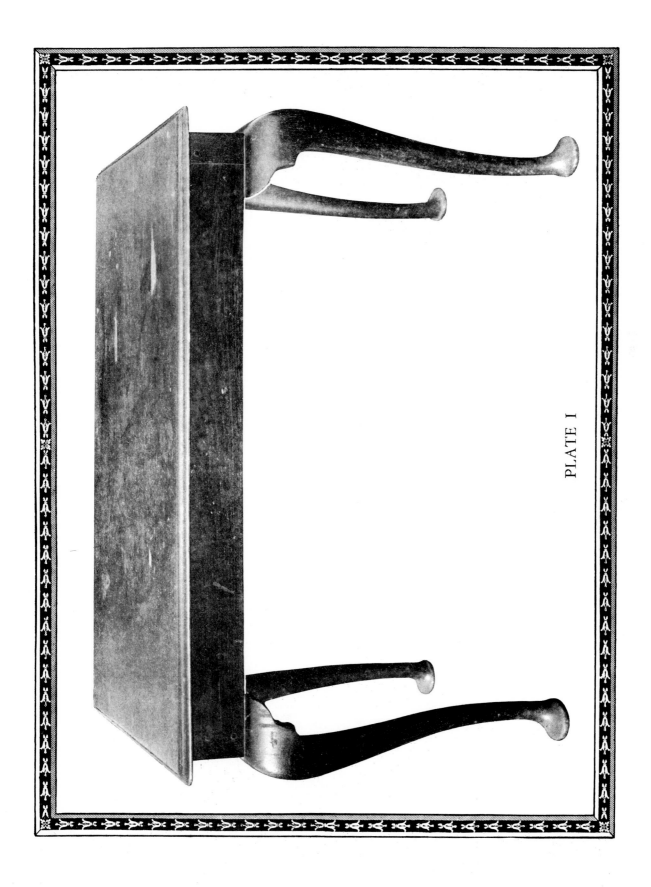

PLATE I

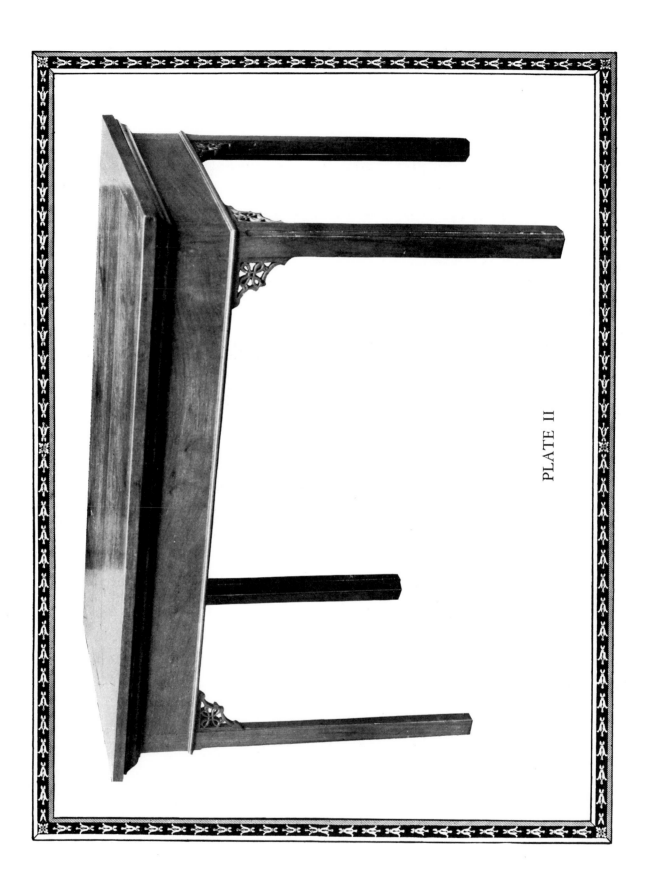

PLATE II

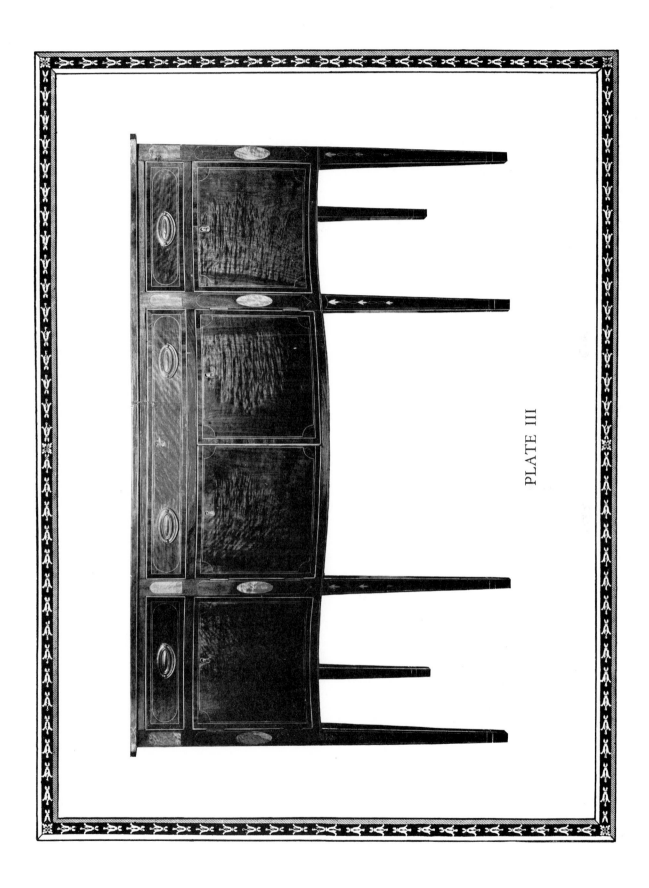

PLATE III

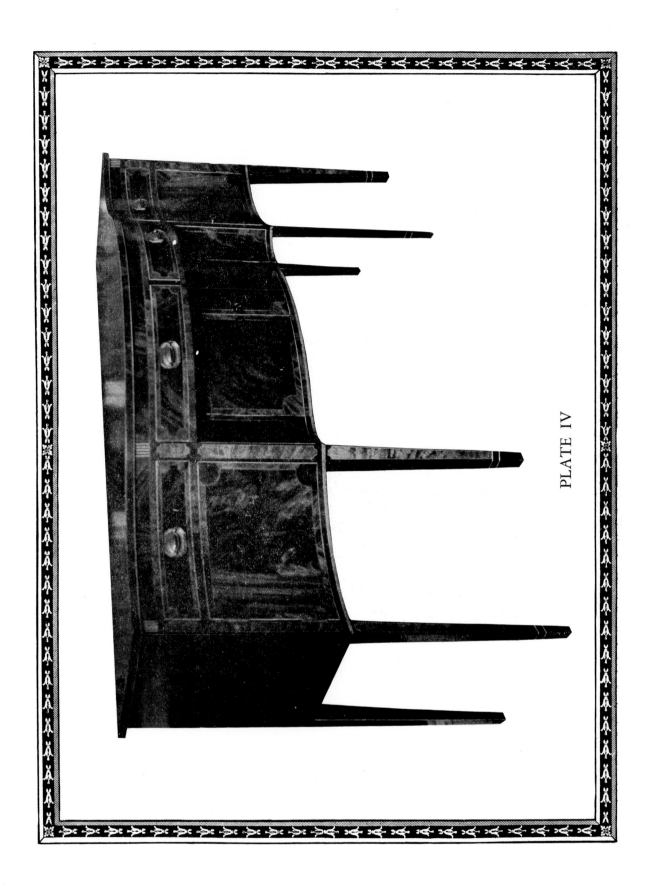

PLATE IV

PLATE V

PLATE VI

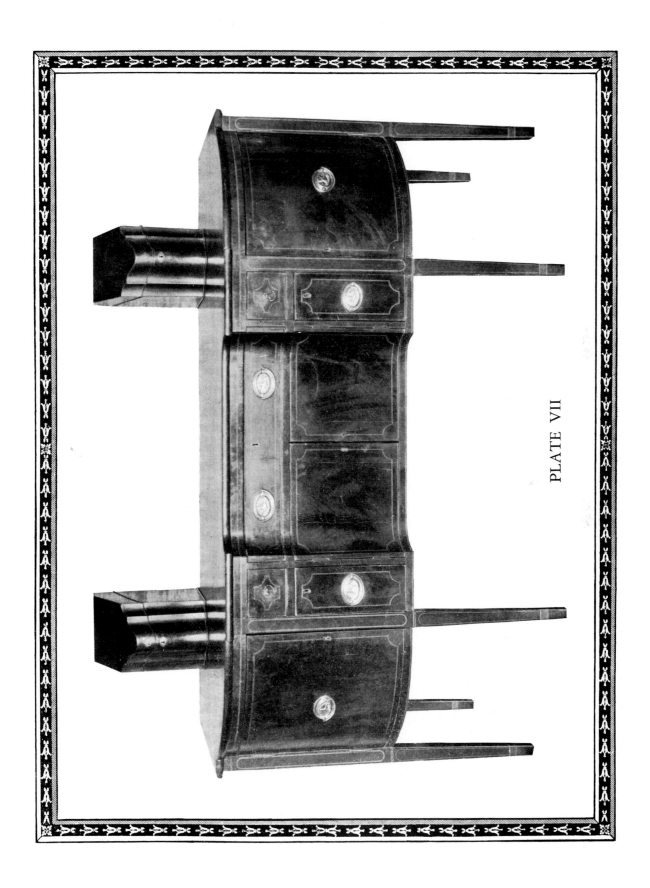

PLATE VII

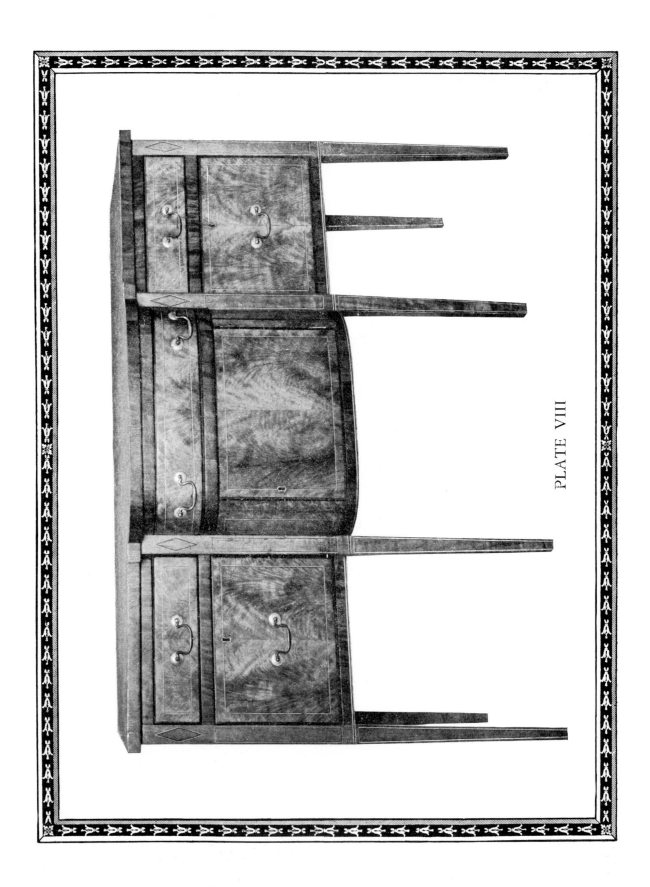

PLATE VIII

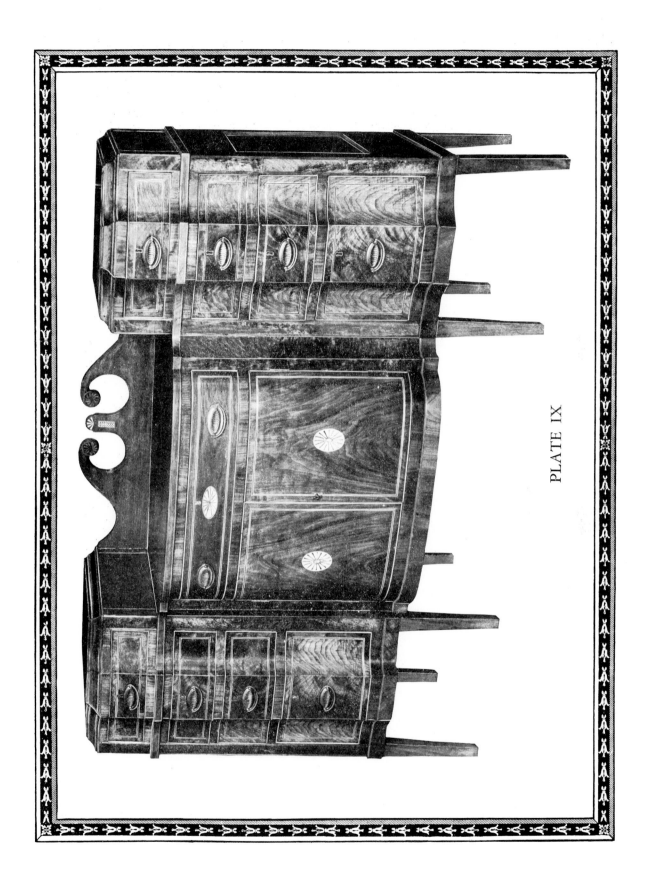

PLATE IX

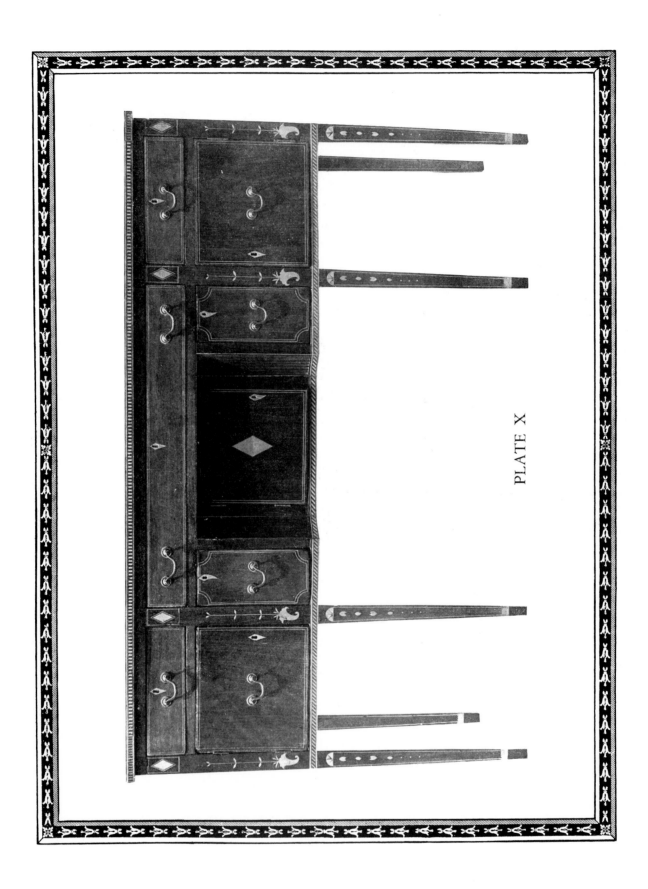

PLATE X

PLATE XI

X

GATE-LEGGED AND DINING TABLES

SINCE the days of King Arthur, a table, and particularly a dining table, has been synonymous with royalty. Often to dine with a man is to make him your friend. The table, perhaps, more than any piece of furniture, serves to bring people into a closer relation and better understanding of each other, and of affairs as well. The interests of the American colonists were few, and they depended, to a great extent, on what they received in the way of pleasure, in their homes and from each other. It was around some of the tables that this pleasure found its best expression.

Washington's dinners, while he was President, were stately affairs, from which the ladies retired after the cloth had been removed, to await the gentlemen in the drawing-room above. Heavy dinners were the rule, with fish and fowl, pies, puddings, fruit and jellies a part of the general scheme. Jefferson gave dinner parties every day at Washington when Congress was being held, where from fourteen to eigh-

teen sat down as soon as it ended its daily session. The dinner bell at Monticello rang at five o'clock. Tea was served in the evening.

The picture further back of the Southern pioneer, in his rudely constructed house in a cleared space in the forest, seated in his great wainscot chair at the head of his "dining bord" as it was called, with his family around him on benches and stools, is pleasing to us. The first table used in America, we are told, was the large rectangular table, the type used before 1675, in the South, of carved oak, and made with bulbous legs, six or four as the number may have been, showing turnings akin to those of the old cupboard of 1620, and relating itself to the old refectory or trestle tables in use in the English monasteries of former days.

Another table, however, was to assume the first place of importance before the end of the seventeenth century. This was the gate-leg table, showing a drop-leaf— sometimes called the flap-leaf—to be developed in many forms, and to take many forms of turnings in the days following, as dictated by the inward promptings of the craftsman at work.

The gate-leg table has a long history of beauty and usefulness. Originating in the spiral twist of English design in the middle of the seventeenth century, it has shown much variety in style and form. As popular and decorative as this table is today, it is hard to realize that it reaches back into

Early dining table

the South of stormy times, when the colonists lived in fear of the Indians lurking at their door, and the men of the house came back from the long struggles to tell their stories around this table. It is true, however, that the majority of the gate-legs were used as dining tables—those with eight legs undoubtedly so.

It is a highly desired type by collectors today. The square stretcher in the table

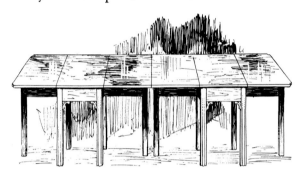

Two-section Chippendale dining table

indicates its Southern origin, although many are found with the Southern pine drawer lining, and well turned stretchers. The smaller gate-legs, made for all purposes where a conveniently sized table that could be folded up when not in use was needed, are rare.

About 1720, the period of Queen Anne, the cabriole-leg table, with two drop-leaves and swinging legs, came into being. These had square, round, and oval tops with four and six legs. Three-section tables were first made in this period, and showed the square drop-leaf center, and the two half-moon ends with four legs, one leg on each end swinging to support a leaf. Due to the large size of the dining rooms in the Southern mansions, the majority of these three-section tables are found here, popular be-

cause the ends might serve as side tables when not in use, but when larger seating capacity was needed, could be put to immediate use.

The Chippendale style yields very few examples of the three-section type, and these show the square, thumb-print legs, rather than the claw-and-ball foot. An example of a Chippendale three-section with square legs is shown, when closed, having three legs at each end. The sketch of the two-section table having corner brackets, and of this period, and was found by the author in the Broad River district of South Carolina.

Many examples of the two- and three-section tables in the Hepplewhite style are found, some of them very elaborately inlaid. The specimens illustrated are unquestionably of Southern workmanship. The use of walnut having practically disappeared in the latter part of the Hepplewhite period, we find, with the Sheraton and Empire, many fine examples in mahogany. The early Empire produced the pedestal table of the tripod type in two- and three-

*Sheraton two-section dining table
with D-shape ends*

sections, having the brass lion's-paw feet. The later Empire, about 1825, produced pieces that were extremely heavy, often showing over-ornamentation.

PLATES

PLATE I. SLIDING GATE-LEG TABLE— WALNUT. (Virginia—c. 1700). This type of the sliding gate-leg table of Southern origin is very rare, and one that has not been given the recognition due it. The turnings resemble many of the swinging gate-leg types found throughout the South. Two of them have been found in the same section. No others are known to exist. If this was imported into the South from elsewhere in the colonies, the imputation is that there should be others known. Although of more fragile construction than the swinging gate-leg, it has considerable merit of design. (Photograph, courtesy of Mrs. J. L. Brockwell).

PLATE II. GATE-LEG TABLES WITH A VARIETY OF TURNINGS AND WOODS. (c. all about 1700). Large tables likely used as dining tables. Top—A fine, heavily turned gate-leg, one of the finest found in the South. Right—The table shows peculiar turnings of the bell-and-trumpet type, found on early highboys. Three of these tables with same turnings have found their way into the hands of one dealer. Left— The table shown here is with turnings of a design of which many are found. As shown, the feet are missing. Bottom—This table is very close in approach to the "Bobbin"-turned English table. Its construction is of native fruit wood.

PLATE III. QUEEN ANNE THREE-SECTION TABLE—WALNUT. (North Carolina—c. 1710-1740). This, the first of the three-section type of table, is very rare, and its age speaks for itself. It is thought to have originated in central North Carolina. Three are definitely known to have been found in Mecklenburg County, and the type is rarely found anywhere else in the Southern states. The extreme rarity of the type may account for this. Parts of such types are often found, but one complete is rarely heard of.

PLATE IV. CHIPPENDALE CLAW-AND-BALL-FOOT TABLE—WALNUT. (North Carolina—c. 1760-1770). This table may have been part of a two- or three-section table, but as such tables are sometimes found with round leaves, it could well be a dining table complete in itself. Attention is called to the crosspiece that is shown underneath the table, exposed by the swinging leg. The wide grain of Southern pine is almost visible in this plate. Oak is sometimes used for such constructions, but the finding of Southern pine in the construction substantiates Southern origin. (Property of Mrs. Paul Chatham).

PLATE V. CHIPPENDALE THREE-SECTION DINING TABLE—MAHOGANY. (South Carolina—c. 1780). Here is shown a late Chippendale dining table with square legs, not tapered, and a six-leg center. This type of table when closed, shows three legs on the ends of the center sections. The center leg is stationary, and two legs swing to support two leaves from each side. These tables are sometimes exceptionally wide, and some have been found measuring fifty-four inches across, although the general width throughout the various styles is around forty-eight inches. (Property of J. K. Beard).

PLATE VI. HEPPLEWHITE THREE-SEC-TION TABLE—WALNUT. (South Carolina—c. 1790). This table shows a type of the three-section tables, many of which are found in the South, made from walnut and mahogany, with square, tapered legs. Those inlaid with the bellflower design are not common. More elaborately inlaid tables are found than the one illustrated, but this

is a representative type. (Property of Mrs. M. A. Robbins).

PLATE VII. EARLY EMPIRE THREE-SECTION DINING TABLE — MAHOGANY. (Virginia—c. 1810-1820). Tables of this type, with the rope-twist legs, are often referred to by dealers as English tables, but very few are found in England. The rope-twist, spoken of as late Sheraton, was used in Sheraton's last book of designs. The brass cup and casters on the leg indicate the early Empire period. The style of leg shown is found on all types of furniture made at this time, and was evidently very popular.

PLATE I

PLATE II

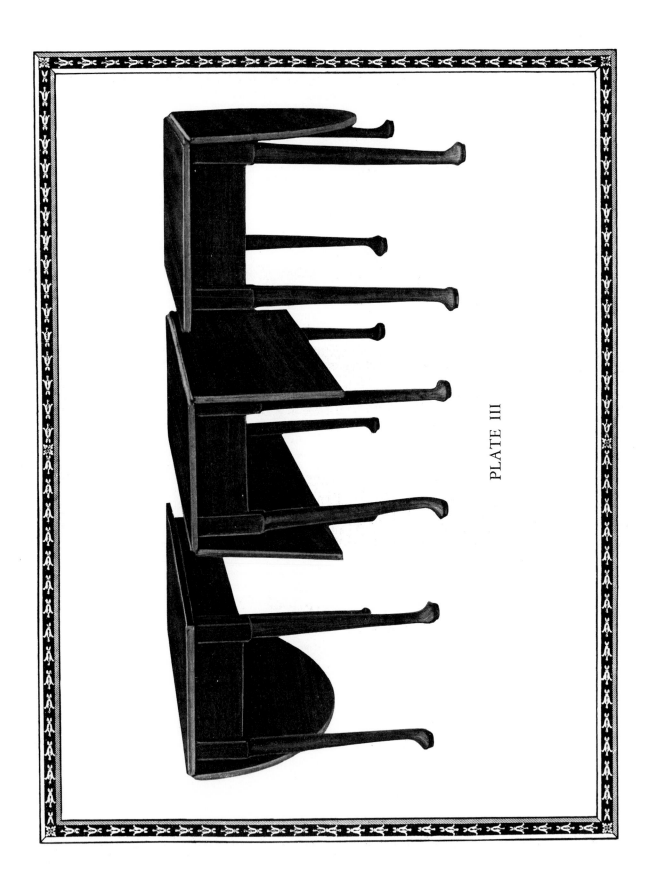

PLATE III

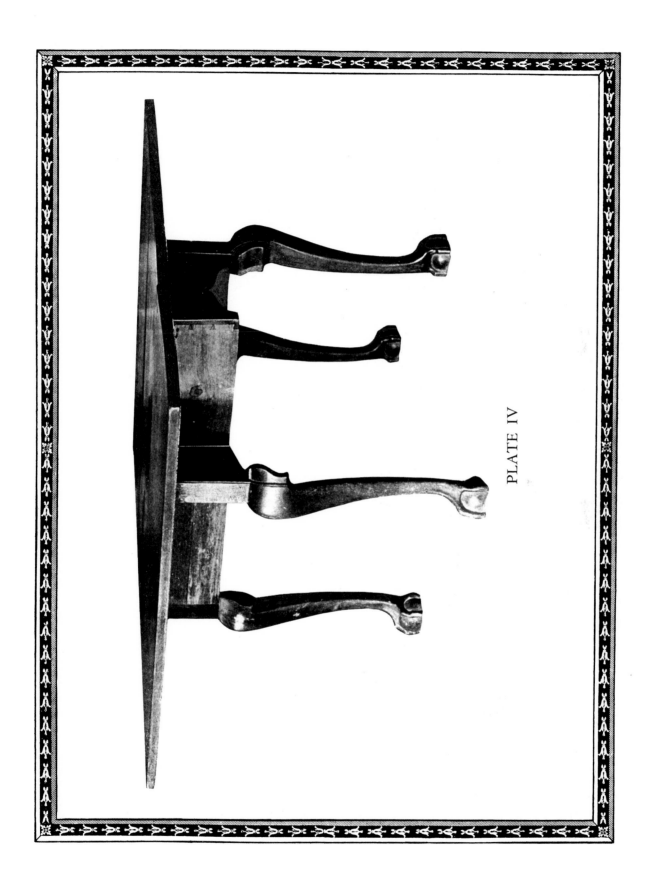

PLATE IV

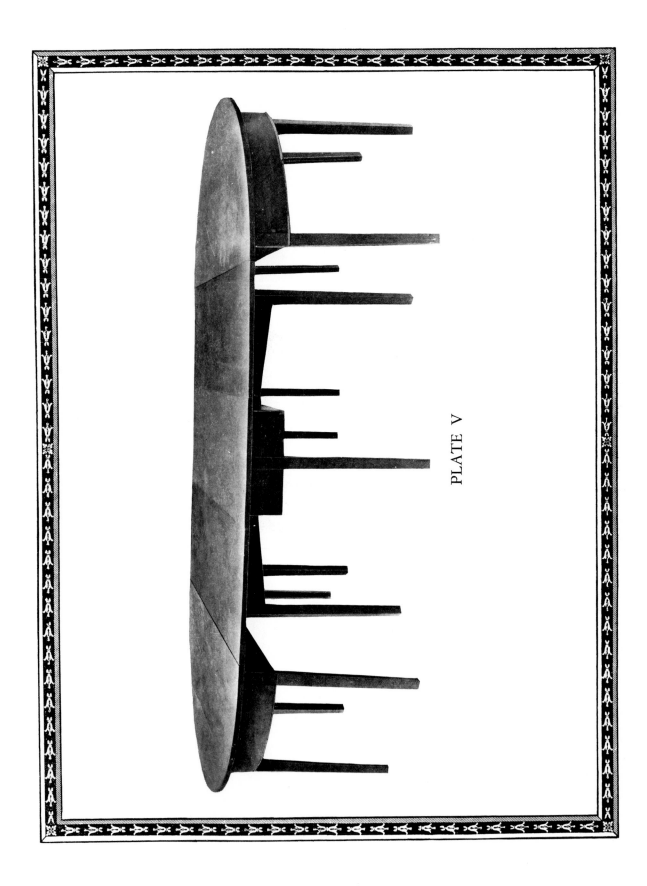

PLATE V

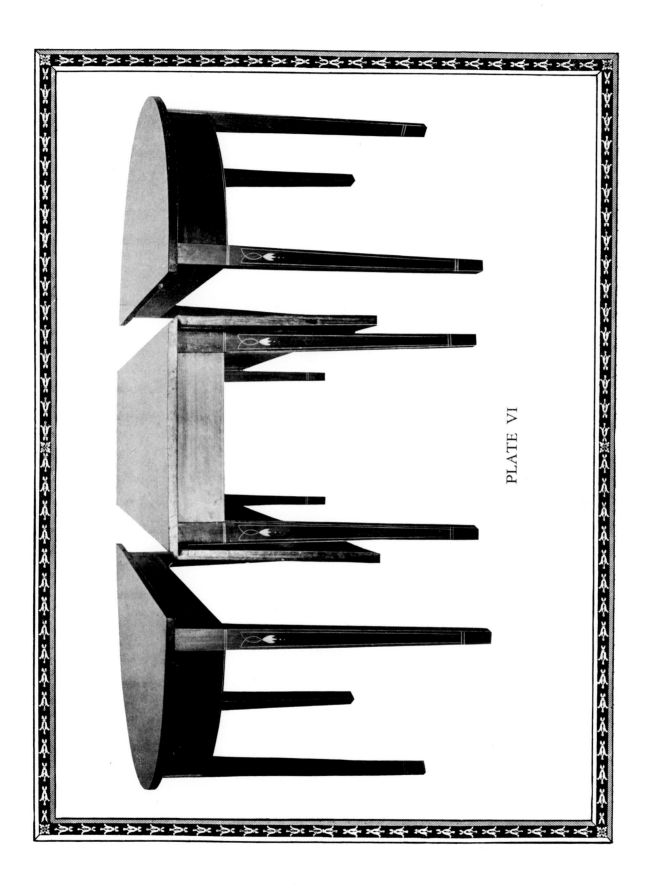

PLATE VI

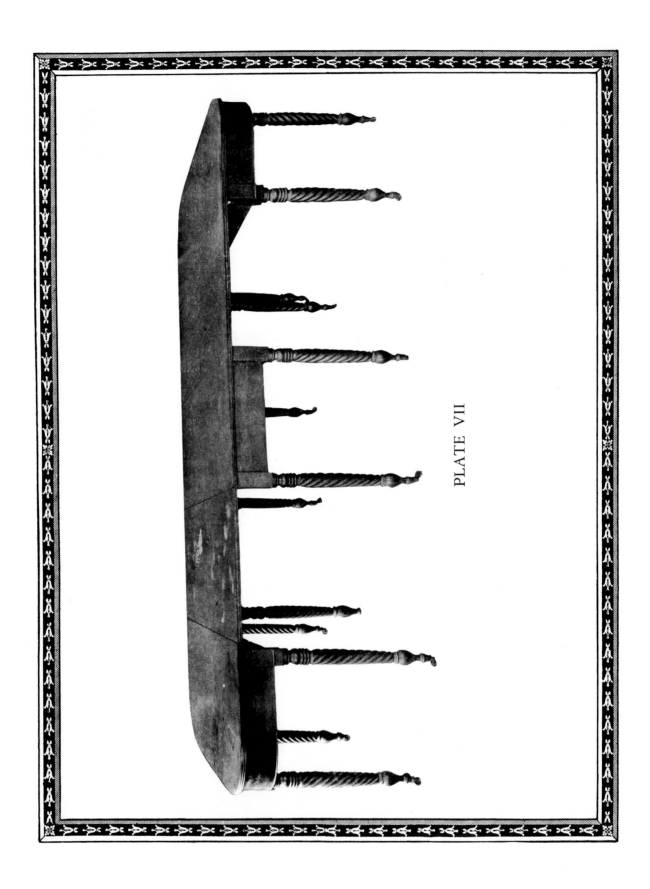

PLATE VII

XI

HUNTING BOARDS

THE hunting boards around which the owners of Southern plantations gathered their friends before and after the hunt, resemble the sideboard in plan and execution, and served to some degree the same purpose. They were often in plain designs, and served as a part of the equipment of the homes. With the Southern

forests rich with game and the housewife eager for the results of the day's hunt, the sport was indulged in by all classes. The richer homes displayed finer types, with the Hepplewhite and Sheraton influence at

work on the best of them, and some of them, unusually well made, were prize pieces. As a general rule, they are taller than the sideboards, and their design leads one to believe that they were used chiefly in halls where members of the hunt could stand and partake of wine and food in the fashion of a buffet lunch. The sketches show plain types found in the rural sections.

PLATES

PLATE I. CHIPPENDALE SIDE TABLE—WALNUT. (Virginia—c. 1770). A large table that might have been used for the purpose of a hunting board. It shows Chippendale influence; in fact, almost an exact copy of one of his plates. (Property of Joe Kindig, Jr.).

PLATE II. HEPPLEWHITE HUNTING BOARD OR SILVER TABLE—WALNUT. (North Carolina—c. 1770-1785). A felt top on this Hepplewhite hunting board suggests that it might have been put to use as a silver table. The legs are square and chamfered, indicating that the Chippendale influence had extended itself into the '80's on this board. Some question arises as to the handles in the piece. This matter is a debatable one. This piece shows the wine drawer in the center. (Property of Mrs. J. L. Brockwell).

PLATE III. HEPPLEWHITE HUNTING BOARD OR TABLE—WALUNT. (Virginia—c. 1790). This is a particularly fine table of the hunting board class. Showing the approximate height and depth of the hunting table, it is so designated. The spade foot is employed. The legs are inlaid with mahogany panels. (Property of J. Pope Nash).

PLATE IV. TOP—SHERATON HUNTING BOARD OR SIDEBOARD—WALNUT. (South Carolina—c. 1790-1800. This type of sideboard, or hunting board, is found in considerable numbers throughout the South. This piece presents the style of sideboard used by the tradesmen, middle-men and small planters in the period. It is a well-made piece, and influenced by the Sheraton design as indicated by the arch center, although the square leg is retained. Other pieces were recorded as made in this style as late as 1815. One dated as made 1812 has been found. Many such plain sideboards are found, while there are others showing elaborate inlay. This board has the wine drawer in one end. (Property of Mrs. B. P. Hodgman).

PLATE IV. BOTTOM—HUNTING BOARD—PINE. (North Carolina—c. 1800-1830). A hunting board of the plain type, with moldings resembling the early chests. Dates on pieces of this type are difficult to determine, but they were made late. (Property of W. S. Ahern).

PLATE V. TOP—SHERATON HUNTING BOARD—MAHOGANY. (Georgia—c. 1800). The cut of this finely-made hunting board of the later period is somewhat indistinct, but the legs are nicely reeded, and have the carved leaf design in the tops, a design which has been found also in tables and sideboards. (Property of Francis D. Brinton).

PLATE V. BOTTOM—EARLY EMPIRE HUNTING BOARD—MAHOGANY. (South Carolina—c. 1810-1830). The large reeding in this piece reflects the tendency of the period of making its furniture larger in size. Pieces of this type, however, are not plentiful.

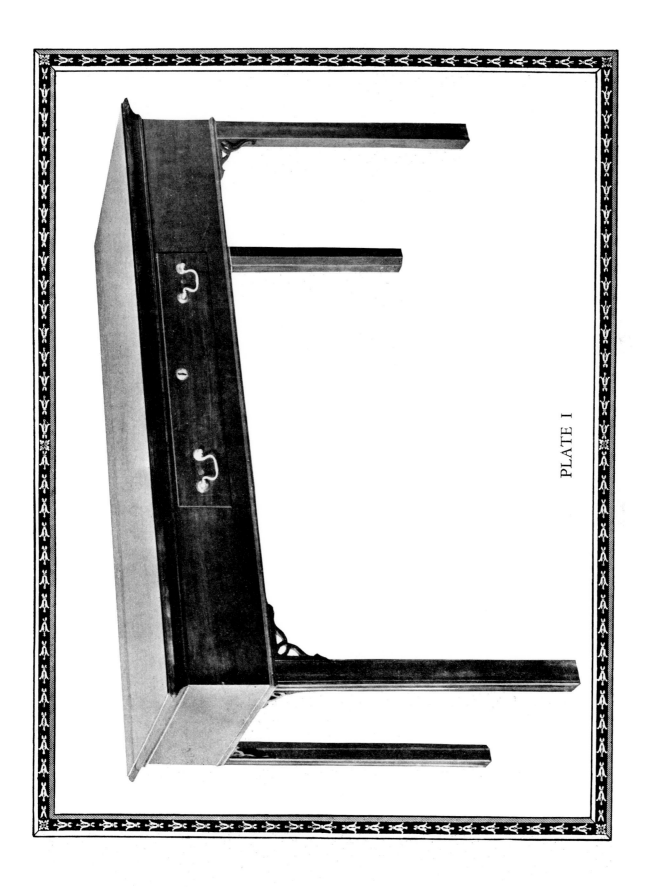

PLATE I

PLATE II

PLATE III

PLATE IV

PLATE V

XII

CELLARETS

THE cellaret is the most peculiarly Southern piece of all furniture. It came into use following the advent of the bottling of wines; and the majority of specimens that have been found are in Chippendale and Hepplewhite styles, with an occasional Queen Anne or earlier example to be noted. They were made com-

Empire cellarets and liquor case

plete in themselves with a drawer, a mixing slide, and spaces for eight, ten, and twelve bottles; and this characteristic piece of furniture in its various forms is found in great quantities throughout the South, and

rarely elsewhere. It is an item often overlooked by collectors.

The word cellaret, in its real meaning, refers to an article of furniture used for cooling wines; but it has come to designate a liquor case or wine cabinet. This use is erroneous, but it is found to be the word most widely accepted, by collectors and dealers, to refer to the different types of wine cabinets as they appear.

At no time was the Southern gentleman freer in his hospitality than in the disposal of his drinks. In South Carolina, Madeira, wine and punch were the common drinks, where, as Hewat says, few gentlemen were without "claret, port and other wines." Everywhere it was the same.

PLATES

PLATE I. STRETCHER-BASE CELLARET —WALNUT. (North Carolina—c. 1690-1700). An example of the cellaret reaching back into the seventeenth century. This is of the earliest type, and very rare. Notice is directed to the turning as compared to Plate I, Chapter XIII. This date as given is not too early, as cellarets were made occasionally in England at this date. (Property of Mrs. J. G. Hayes).

PLATE II. TOP—QUEEN ANNE CELLARET—WALNUT. (North Carolina—c. 1710-1740). Little doubt as to the use of this piece as a liquor chest or cellaret is felt, as it is in the original condition, with partitions intact. The early cellaret was built low as compared to those of later periods. The cabriole leg is shown here with a foot of modified Spanish type. (Property of Mrs. J. J. McDevitt).

PLATE II. BOTTOM—QUEEN ANNE CELLARET OR SUGAR CHEST—WALNUT. (South Carolina—c. 1720-1750). This piece of later date than the one illustrated at top, may have been a sugar chest adapted in later years as a cellaret. The decorations of fans in the front, and the slipper-shaped foot, are interesting features. These types are rarely found. (Property of Ralph P. Hanes).

PLATE III. CHIPPENDALE CELLARET— WALNUT. (South Carolina—c. 1760-1770). This cellaret illustrates the fact that Southern workmen were followers of Chippendale, even to the Chinese influence in his design. On the front of this piece are employed raised scrolls similar to those to be found on various cupboards. The owner's initials, inlaid, the mixing slide on the side, and the shaped cross-stretcher and cut-out corner brackets make this piece unique. (Property of Mrs. J. A. Haskell).

PLATE IV. CHIPPENDALE-HEPPLE-WHITE CELLARET—WALNUT. (Virginia— c. 1770-1780). The influence of both Chippendale and Hepplewhite is in the making of this liquor chest. The Hepplewhite is responsible for the fluted legs, while the corner brackets and square legs chamfered on the inside, belong to the Chippendale style. The mixing slide without the drawer is found from this time until 1800. The legs are fluted. This fluting is not to be

confused with the term reeded, which applies to the half-round raised decorations found on legs of later furniture. (Property of Joe Kindig, Jr.).

PLATE V. HEPPLEWHITE CELLARET— MAHOGANY. (North Carolina—c. 1780-1800). An inlaid mahogany piece, with the square, tapered legs characteristic of the Hepplewhite and Sheraton style, which shows a cellaret that was made in quantity throughout the Southern states. The quality was governed by the skill of the workman attempting the piece. The ovals of inlay with the urn and flowers are to be noted. (Property of Carroll H. Fowlkes).

PLATE VI. HEPPLEWHITE CELLARET— WALNUT. (Virginia—c. 1790-1800). This Hepplewhite cellaret, one of a pair found about thirty miles from each other, and owned by different families. They were not made as a pair, but came from the hands of the same workman. There is a slight variation in size between them. Attention is called to the inlaid oval on the front of the chest, a type of inlay used on many pieces throughout the South and a clever, though humble imitation of the ovals found on elaborate pieces. The black parts shown in the oval were made of colored putty and cut out after the oval had been put into the wood, with a gouge. They were then filled with colored putty instead of being made of wood. This was often done, too, with the more elaborate pieces. Thus the workman was given opportunity with a variety of decoration that could be made, as a rule, only with curved sides. (Property of Mrs. George L. Street).

PLATE I

PLATE II

PLATE III

PLATE IV

PLATE V

PLATE VI

XIII
TABLES

TEA drinking was introduced into the colonies in an early period, and became popular in the South. Card playing was perhaps the chief diversion of the men, and women likewise indulged in the sport. The almost pressing need for tables for such purposes made tea and card tables in abundance a necessity; but their use was not always confined to the purpose for which they were made, serving as they did for breakfast and supper table. These tables were a combination of charm and convenience.

The only tables made especially for tea drinking were those with the raised rim or gallery, to prevent the china, fragile as it was, from slipping off the table. The exceptionally small gate-leg table served the purpose of a tea table admirably. Tea tables are mentioned in inventories as early as 1722, during which period were made tavern tables with splayed legs, making them difficult to tip over. Claypoole, in South Carolina, in 1740, made "all sorts of tea tables." The first real table having a raised rim made its appearance in the Queen Anne period. It is a type of old table rarely found today; but it is a popular style used by modern manufacturers.

The butterfly table, a solely American design, is said never to have been found outside of New England, but one purchased in Columbia, South Carolina, a few years ago, of the trestle type, as shown by sketch, was examined in the course of this study and found to be made of Southern walnut throughout, with Southern pine used in the crossbar underneath the top. This table is now in a prominent collection. Proof may be adduced from the finding of this table that traveling cabinet-makers came South very early.

In the Chippendale period came what is known as the pie-crust table. This had a scalloped top with raised rim, set upon

Walnut butterfly table

a tripod. These are also very rare. The English tables of this type were elaborately carved, but the Southern examples are plain, and devoid of carving on the knees. The Pembroke table, named presumably for the lady at whose order the first one was made, originated in England at this time. It has four square legs, with a drop-

76

leaf on either side, and served the purpose of a breakfast or supper table. Hepplewhite and Sheraton show tables of this type in very elaborate design, and call them breakfast or supper tables, and those produced by the Southern workmen were chaste and interesting examples of the type. Specimens in the tripod type are found extending into the Empire period; and the later Sheraton examples had brass lion's-paw feet and tilting top.

Many Southern gentlemen combined hard drinking with their other diversions, and were inveterate gamblers, be it known. Piquet, faro, and écarté were the chief games that they played. The ladies and younger men indulged in loo. Card tables needed to be well made, and were especially constructed for the purpose in the eighteenth century; and they were listed in inventories as early as 1727. They took the characteristics of each period in which they were made, and appear in delightful manner in many forms. As distinguished from other tables, they have a flap top, and four or five legs. Peculiar to the majority of Southern-made card tables are the five legs, four of which are stationary, and one of which swings out to support the top when open. Card tables of the Hepplewhite period are sometimes found very elaborately inlaid, and frequently in pairs. Mahogany was the most popular wood for this type of table.

The active interests in the home relate themselves to the small table. To encompass the various tables of small size made in the South, to meet the various needs, would constitute a comprehensive study. One plantation owner is listed as having owned twenty-three. Much ingenuity was employed by the Southern craftsmen to meet the demand. With the gate-leg and its drop-leaf, used for many purposes, on came the procession of the small tables: the tavern early as the gate-leg, with a fine table of the stretcher type shown in this book, followed by a stretcher table of a more elaborate variety; the side table and dressing table; tea and card tables, devoted to many uses; mixing tables; a Windsor table after a more northern type; a host of them were employed. "At the Sign of the Tea Table and Chair in Gay Street," Hopkins in 1767, in Baltimore, was offering a vast array made in mahogany, walnut, and cherry, with carving and without, "card, parlor and tea tables . . . decanter stands, tea kettle stands, dumb waiters and tea boards."

Attention is called to the sewing table. Diversion was afforded, even for women of wealth, in handwork and sewing, and which made the sewing table a piece of importance. Women of all classes took pride in their work. "In the country life of America there are many moments when a woman can have recourse to nothing but her needle," Thomas Jefferson wisely observed, urging his daughter in Paris to perfect herself further in the use of it before her return to Albemarle County. The influence of Chippendale, Hepplewhite and Sheraton and the Empire is seen in the workmanship of these small, Southern tables, and collectors have long been in the field searching out types.

PLATES

PLATE I. Top—Sawbuck or X-Frame Table—Walnut. (North Carolina—c.

1700). This table possesses decorative possibilities that a good joiner could easily have made the most of. The piece shows a decided Pennsylvania German influence. This table is in itself of German design, originating from the earliest type of cross-leg table, and is essentially from the German Gothic of the sixteenth century. This table is rarely found made entirely of walnut. (Property of Ralph P. Hanes).

PLATE I. Bottom—Drop-Leaf Stretcher Table — Walnut. (North Carolina—c. 1700). Another North Carolina table of a rare type, showing slides to support the leaves. The turnings on this table are to be noted. They have the heavy bulbous parts of the leg placed in opposition to the general rule. This has been found to be true on the majority of tables throughout the states below Virginia. Whether this is a distinguishing mark, by which tables made in a certain section may be identified, I cannot say. It sets the work apart as being Southern made. (Property of Ralph P. Hanes).

PLATE II. Top—Queen Anne Tea Table—Walnut. (North Carolina—c. 1730-1750). A tea table of fine proportion and gracefully scrolled apron, and with finely shaped cabriole legs. Although the table illustrated is an excellent one, four-leg tables are found throughout the Southern states—rarely however of this quality. This table has the indented corner top.

PLATE II. Bottom—Queen Anne Dish-Top Tea Table—Walnut. (North Carolina—c. 1730-1750). This charming dish-top table, although not embellished with carving, has exceedingly graceful lines. It is unquestionably a tea table, showing the raised rim, to prevent dishes from sliding off. The general effect of this table may be secured by applying a rim to a plain table. With fakers at work already, according to the plan, in buying it would be well to make certain that the dished effect, or rim, is cut from the solid wood, rather than applied. (Property of Mrs. J. L. Brockwell).

PLATE III. Top—Oval Top Splay-Leg Table—Walnut. (Virginia—c. 1720-1740). This table, with the canted legs, is often called a tavern table. The example shown is a fine specimen. The feet are very similar to the modified type of Spanish foot found on the many Pennsylvania pieces known as the drake foot. The ogee scroll, noticeable in the apron of this table, is a decorative feature used by skilled cabinetmakers in this period. (Property of Joe Kindig, Jr.).

PLATE III. Bottom—Claw-and-Ball Foot Table—Walnut. (Virginia—c. 1750-1780). This table resembles the one shown at the top, but of a later date and lighter construction, with a gracefully scrolled apron. (Property of J. Pope Nash).

PLATE IV. Chippendale Pie-Crust Table—Walnut. (Virginia—c. 1760-1770). The Chippendale pie-crust table is an unusually popular type. Because of its early appeal to collectors, it is now very rare. Particular attention is called to the rim of this table, since the moulding seems to have been planed down. As a rule, this type of table has a raised moulding carved from the solid wood; but the owner is authority for the statement that he has had three with rims similar to this one, and that all came from the same section. The table within itself is a unique type. In seeking to discover whether or not the tops of tables of this type are original, the shrinkage of the wood may be taken into consideration, as that, as time wears on, causes a table top to be slightly shorter in diameter opposite the grain than across the diameter with the grain. (Property of J. K. Beard).

PLATE V. Top—Chippendale Pie-Crust Table—Mahogany. (Virginia—c. 1760-1775). Pie-crust tables bought out of the South, have been said by Mr. Kindig to have shorter scallops in the rim than the Philadelphia type; and the majority of them to have a turned column in the shape of the one shown. The number of English tables brought into this country in the last few years is so fast overwhelming the American product that a study of this type, from the standpoint of American workmanship, will shortly be out of the question. (Property of Joe Kindig, Jr.).

PLATE V. Bottom — Chippendale Pembroke Table—Mahogany. (North Carolina—c. 1770-1790). A late Pemboke-style table with Chippendale characteristics, and a rare type, having the cross stretchers and bowed ends. Tables of this style and period are found with serpentine-shaped ends and shaped drop-leaves. (Property of Miss Elizabeth Thompson).

PLATE VI. Top—Hepplewhite Pembroke Table—Mahogany. (South Carolina—c. 1790). This finely inlaid Pembroke table, with the oval top and bowed ends, shows the Hepplewhite influence. This type is about forty inches in length with leaves up, and was probably used as a supper or breakfast table. It is a very popular type, and was made in quantities throughout the South, with varying degrees of workmanship employed, and with straight ends and various shaped tops. More tables of this type are found here than in any other section of the colonies. (Property of Mrs. M. A. Robbins).

PLATE VI. Bottom—Hepplewhite Pembroke Table—Mahogany. (Maryland—c. 1790). Another table of the same description as the piece shown at the top, with the leaves down, by way of presenting the shape to better advantage. The bell-flower is worked out in finer design in this than in the top table. As many as thirteen bellflowers, inlaid on the legs of such tables, have been seen. (Property of J. K. Beard).

PLATE VII. Queen Anne Corner Card Tables—Walnut. (Maryland—c. 1730-1750). The triangular form of these tables made them convenient to place in a corner, gave them their name, and made them popular. A pair of tables of this type could also be placed together to make a larger table. Tables of this type are rare, particularly in pairs. All card tables are sought after in pairs. (Property of Francis D. Brinton).

PLATE VIII. TOP—CHIPPENDALE CARD TABLE—MAHOGANY. (Maryland—c. 1770-1790). This table is labeled "John Shaw of Annapolis." There is some question over labeled Shaw pieces, as he was also an importer, but such a table as this could easily have been made by him. (Property of Mrs. Miles White).

PLATE VIII. BOTTOM—CHIPPENDALE CLAW-AND-BALL-FOOT CARD TABLE—MAHOGANY. (South Carolina—c. 1760-1780). The carving on the knees of this claw-and-ball-foot table is very good, and the carving around the skirt is an excellent feature. Such tables are scarce, but many English tables of this type have been imported, at the period this was made, and at the present time.

PLATE IX. CHIPPENDALE CARD TABLE —MAHOGANY. (North Carolina—c. 1780). This card table shows where the workman was influenced by the designs of Chippendale and Hepplewhite. The square, chamfered legs, the serpentine shape, and the carved corner brackets show the influence of Chippendale, while the general light construction and the inlay indicate the designs of Hepplewhite. (Property of Joe Kindig, Jr.).

PLATE X. TOP—HEPPLEWHITE CARD TABLE—MAHOGANY. (South Carolina—c. 1785-1795). A half-round table showing the inlay as explained in Chapter XII, Plate VI. One of a pair of finely made tables with the bellflower. Half-moon tables are found in quantity all over the South. (Property of J. K. Beard).

PLATE X. BOTTOM — HEPPLEWHITE CARD TABLE—MAHOGANY. (Virginia—c. 1785-1795). The five-leg construction is a feature to be noted on Southern card tables. The eagle inlaid furniture, made in every part of the United States, is much sought after. The eagle was a popular motif from 1775 to 1820, as Empire pieces also carried it. Patriotism in America is said to have reached its height following the War of 1812, and the eagle decoration was most popular at this time. (Property of J. K. Beard).

PLATE XI. TOP—SHERATON CARD TABLE—MAHOGANY AND MAPLE. (South Carolina—c. 1800). Here bird's-eye and curly maple have been used on the skirt of this Sheraton card table. The heavy reeding on Southern pieces does not always indicate a late date. The shape of this table is unusual, with the serpentine center. It was found in the vicinity of Greenwood, where a number of pieces of the Sheraton period have been found having bird's-eye maple as a veneer. (Property of Joe Kindig, Jr.).

PLATE XI. BOTTOM—SHERATON CARD TABLE—MAHOGANY. (Maryland—c. 1800). A nicely inlaid table of fine proportion and workmanship. The delicate, reeded legs are a fine feature of this type table. Tables of this shape are often found, but rarely with inlay and such delicate legs. (Property of Mrs. Fred Sampson).

PLATE XII. EMPIRE CARD TABLES—MAHOGANY. (Maryland—c. 1820). Two card tables of the Empire period, influenced in style by the late Sheraton designs. These resemble tables made by Duncan Phyfe, but in the known examples of Phyfe's work the legs have a downward curve starting at the pedestal. The top table has better lines, and the bottom table has finer carving.

PLATE XIII. TOP—TAVERN TABLE—WALNUT. (Virginia—c. 1690-1700). This small tavern table, from a distant day, comes to us in its original condition, and is of marked interest. A fine table of this type in such quality as this possesses, is very rare. Many are found throughout the South, showing a different variety of turnings, but seldom like this. It may have had a larger top. (Property of Mrs. E. M. Crutchfield).

PLATE XIII. BOTTOM—STRETCHER TABLE—WALNUT. (Virginia—c. 1710-1730). This stretcher table, in walnut, shows a little more elaborate construction than that at the top of the page with the turned stretchers and drawer. Delicately turned tables of this type are seldom found today, but many were shown in inventories of that period. One plantation owner in Virginia possessed as many as twenty-three small tables. This number may have included candle stands, as every room had to be supplied with light, and two or more tables were needed in each. Many stretcher tables were made, but few have survived. (Property of Mrs. J. G. Hayes).

PLATE XIV. TOP—WINDSOR-TYPE TABLE—WALNUT. (Virginia—c. 1770-

1790). A turned table of rare style, with turnings resembling the Windsor chair. (Property of Carroll H. Fowlkes).

PLATE XIV. RIGHT—DROP-LEAF STRETCHER TABLE—PINE. (North Carolina—c. 1700-1730). The stretcher with a drop-leaf is shown here. Although larger, it has the characteristics of the butterfly table. The plainly turned legs, which are vertical and not slanted, are unusual, as is the bracket which holds the leaf. The square brace, which holds up the leaf when open, fits into the frame beneath when closed. (Property of Mrs. E. M. Crutchfield).

PLATE XIV. LEFT—CHIPPENDALE MIXING TABLE—WALNUT. (Virginia—c. 1760-1780). This table shows a soapstone top. It was used, without doubt, for the mixing of drinks, a popular pastime of the period; but the soapstone top may have been supplied with the idea of saving the surface or the top from the heat of hot dishes placed upon it. (Property of J. Pope Nash).

PLATE XIV. BOTTOM—STRETCHER TABLE—CHERRY. (North Carolina—c. 1710-1740). This stretcher table, made of cherry, shows heavy turnings for a table of its age. The piece was found in the vicinity of Salem, but represents a period antecedent to that in which the Moravians arrived there. (Property of Ralph P. Hanes).

PLATE XV. TOP—QUEEN ANNE SIDE TABLE—WALNUT. (Virginia—c. 1720-

1750). A fine table of graceful proportion, and beautifully shaped legs. It is so fashioned that it could be used either as a side table or as a dressing table, although dressing tables, as a rule, have more drawer space. Many more crudely made tables of this type are found throughout the South, but examples like the illustration are rare. The corners are indented. (Property of J. F. Geisinger).

PLATE XV. Bottom—CHIPPENDALE SIDE TABLE—WALNUT. (Georgia—c. 1750-1770). This table, with the thumbprint leg and scrolled brackets, is an excellent example of the Chippendale period. The scrolled apron adds a very decorative effect. (Property of Mrs. Fred Sampson).

PLATE XVI. Top—HEPPLEWHITE SERPENTINE SIDE OR DRESSING TABLE—MAHOGANY. (Virginia—c. 1780-1800). A fine table with shaped front. (Property of Carroll H. Fowlkes).

PLATE XVI. Bottom—SHERATON DRESSING TABLE—MAHOGANY. (North Carolina—c. 1790-1810). Although with the tapered inlaid legs, this piece, as indicated by the pulls and the reeded edge of the top, is of the Sheraton period. It is the first of its type to come within the line of this study. It is evident that it was made to be used for the purpose as stated; but such pieces as this are unique, and it serves the average collector to poor purpose to search for them, except that his searchings may lead to some other type equally unique. The dressing tables, produced in cabinetmaking centers, with lifting top enclosing a mirror and numerous compartments, which are gems of a craftsman's art, are rarely found today. (Property of Ralph P. Hanes).

PLATE XVII. Top—HEPPLEWHITE CARD OR SIDE TABLE—WALNUT. (North Carolina—c. 1790-1800). Ingenious construction is shown in this table having five legs of a very unique design, the fifth leg folding behind one of the other. The flap top and fifth leg appear as if an afterthought on the part of the maker. The drawers in this type of table are unusual. Attention is called to the design in the inlay made in the manner described in Chapter XII. Tables without the flap top and extra leg of this type are found throughout the Southern states, with varying degrees of elaboration by use of inlay. (Property of Mrs. A. G. Ryland).

PLATE XVII. Bottom—HEPPLEWHITE STAND—WALNUT. (North Carolina—c. 1790-1800). Small stands in great quantity are found throughout the South in this shape. The use of the single bellflower is to be noted, as used on all types of Southern-made furniture. Found in Mecklenburg County, where several tables with this inlay have been found. (Property of Mrs. Robert M. Pulliam).

PLATE XVIII. HEPPLEWHITE MIXING TABLE—WALNUT. (Virginia—c. 1790). This piece was found in the Valley of Virginia. The vine inlay displayed in the legs is typical of the influence of the Dutch and German craftsmen who worked there. This type of inlay is found on furniture made in this period in the Shenandoah Valley. On account of this table having a slate top, it is thought to have been used for mixing purposes, presumably for liquor, although there is no partitioning for bottles. (Property of Charles Watkins).

PLATE XIX. TOP—SHERATON SEWING TABLE—CURLY MAPLE. (Virginia—c. 1800). A finely made sewing table of nicely figured wood, showing a type seldom seen in the South. If fashioned in the South, it was done by one who knew the use of curly maple; and this is likely, as the wood, at the beginning of the nineteenth century had come into demand, due to the importation of Northern products into the South. (Property of W. S. Ahern).

PLATE XIX. BOTTOM—SHERATON SEWING TABLE—MAHOGANY. (South Carolina—c. 1800). This Sheraton table was made in the style used by Duncan Phyfe, of New York. The veneering and carving on this table are of the highest quality. The reeding resembles tambour work. The compartments inside the lid, which lifts up, are of satinwood. (Property of Mrs. R. G. Cabell).

PLATE XX. CANDLE STAND AND SEWING TABLES — CURLY MAPLE AND RED CHERRY. (North Carolina—c. 1825). This candle stand is of Hepplewhite design, of a popular type, and made later than the period. The stands were made about the same time by Jacob Siewers, who worked in Salem from 1820 to 1850, and employed a number of cabinetmakers in his shop. The owners of the pieces are the granddaughters of Jacob Siewers. (Property of the Misses Pfhol).

PLATE XXI. TOP—QUEEN ANNE FOLDING TABLE—WALNUT. (South Carolina—c. 1720-1750). A table that folds, and when closed is about three inches in depth. It is a unique piece with legs rather crudely shaped. (Property of Mrs. Gabriel Cannon).

PLATE XXI. LEFT CENTER—QUEEN ANNE CANDLE STANDS—WALNUT. (c. 1740-1780). Two stands of a type found throughout the South, made over a period of about fifty years.

PLATE XXI. RIGHT CENTER—HEPPLEWHITE CANDLE STAND—MAHOGANY. (c. 1780-1810). A popular type made in the Hepplewhite and Sheraton periods throughout the South.

PLATE XXI. LOWER LEFT—EMPIRE CANDLE STAND—MAHOGANY. (South Carolina—c. 1810-1820). An elaborately carved stand with the lion's-paw feet and carved pedestal. (Property of Mrs. Gabriel Cannon).

PLATE XXI. LOWER RIGHT—QUEEN ANNE TABLE—MAHOGANY. (Virginia—c. 1730-1750). A type used for breakfast or supper tables, and rarely found in mahogany. (Property of Mrs. G. Edmond Massie).

PLATE I

PLATE II

PLATE III

PLATE IV

PLATE V

PLATE VI

PLATE VII

PLATE VIII

PLATE IX

PLATE X

PLATE XI

PLATE XII

PLATE XIII

PLATE XIV

PLATE XV

PLATE XVI

PLATE XVII

PLATE XVIII

PLATE XIX

PLATE XX

PLATE XXI

XIV

DESKS AND SECRETARIES

CERTAINLY as far as the South is concerned, the desk is its most distinguished piece of furniture when the uses to which it was put are recalled. Washington, Jefferson, Mason, Madison, and Monroe spent much of their time at their desks, writing state papers and the

Carved Bible box

many interminable letters of that day that had to do with public affairs.

The term desk, now in general use in America, denotes any object of furniture used for writing purposes. Bureau, the English term for an inclosed writing cabinet, is one of the many names for the desk. The modern use of the word, secretary, is from the French word, *scriptoire,* meaning to write, and *scrutoire.* Secretary, today, means a desk with a bookcase top.

The origin of the slant-top desk is the simple Bible box. This box was used as a stand to hold the Bible, or on which to write, and was made from various native

woods. The few found in the South are made of oak, decorated with carving. The early colonial gentleman must, of course, learn to write, particularly with long letters to be sent back to England, and the Bible box was put upon a stand and made to take the form of a desk. In 1690 a chest, with a top having a solid fall board, enclosing drawers and pigeonholes, came into use. This was one of the forerunners of the secretary. Few of this type are known in the South, and those few are of English origin.

In the first half of the eighteenth century, the desk took many forms. The slant-top desk, with drawers below, was the most popular, and continued so with the char-

Fall-front desk

acteristics of each period until 1800. The Queen Anne, with cabriole leg, came in the first quarter of the eighteenth century along with the desks on stretcher frames. Southern examples are found.

Among the various types of desks employed at the beginning of the second quarter of the eighteenth century was the secretary-desk, consisting of a book-

Desk on frame

case resting on a slant-top desk. In the hands of Chippendale it became a thing of beauty; and Southern cabinet-makers did not fail to grasp some of its possibilities. Secretaries with arched tops and ogee feet became popular. Cabinets with serpentine drawer fronts were a favorite design. Walnut, in most instances, with mahogany at times, was employed to fine effect. Walnut was, in fact, the favor-

ite wood in all states except Maryland, until the middle of the eighteenth century, when mahogany came into full sway. The finest pieces after 1750 were mahogany.

The influence of Hepplewhite and Sheraton were felt about 1795, and pleased as Southern craftsmen were with the classic line and more delicate ornamentation, they inlaid their pieces, and many slant-top desks are found with French feet. Many tambour desks and tables for writing purposes, made in the South, show the influence of these two English designers. Rural furniture makers even tried hard to reproduce the designs of Hepplewhite and Sheraton in native woods, as shown in this book. Another form of secretary was popular at the beginning of the nineteenth century. It resembled a chest of drawers with a bookcase top. The top drawer was very deep, and enclosed a writing cabinet. This style had appeared in the South as early as 1750. Southern secretaries became heavy under the Empire influence. The work, however, was of a high order.

It may be noted that the demand among collectors today for small desks not over thirty-six inches in width, is open to question. There is no reason apparent why such selection should be made. The choice of a desk for fine workmanship and good quality does not depend on its being small. Many small desks have poor cabinets; in many cases improved by fakers. Many of the so-called small desks were originally large, and cut down to meet the requirements of the trade. A further question is, whether, in actually buying the desk, the collector is able to distinguish the actual width of what he is after when the piece is placed in a large room, without measuring it.

PLATES

PLATE I. CHILD'S SLANT-TOP DESK WITH WELL —WALNUT. (Virginia—c. 1720-1730). Here is an early walnut piece, with the double-arch moulding around the drawers. Single-arch moulding was of an earlier date. The well compartment, as it is known, is the compartment beneath the writing surface of the desk, covered by a sliding lid, which is part of the floor of the cabinet. The brasses, which are also original, help to set the date on this piece. Small pieces such as this, built especially for children, or as models, are much sought for. This desk was found in a negro cabin on the Rappahannock River. (Property of Mrs. E. M. Crutchfield).

PLATE II. PANELED-DOOR SECRETARY WITH WELL—WALNUT. (North Carolina —c. 1740). This secretary, built with a well, shows an exceptionally fine cabinet for the type that it represents. This early secretary, as the date indicates, was made in the Queen Anne period, but does not show any of the marked characteristics of that period, except perhaps the shell in the interior. The size of this type varies from thirty-six to forty-two inches in width. The smaller size is, of course, the most sought after, but they are rarely found with so fine a cabinet. (Property of Mrs. Robert M. Pulliam).

PLATE III. TOP—QUEEN ANNE DESK —WALNUT. (North Carolina—c. 1710-1740). This type Queen Anne desk, which

is in fact a desk on frame, and a style from which many modern desks are copied, is rare, and few are found. Due to this, the type is often faked by placing the top of a short desk on a table frame. (Property of Joe Kindig, Jr.).

PLATE III. BOTTOM—KNEE-HOLE DESK—WALNUT. (c. 1750-1760). Although this desk is believed to be of English origin, and the drawers are lined with oak, it is illustrated to show the type, and mainly because it was the property of Patrick Henry, Virginia's patriot, orator, and soldier. Desks of the knee-hole type are found throughout the South. (Property of J. Pope Nash).

PLATE IV. CHIPPENDALE DESK—WALNUT. (Virginia—c. 1760-1770). This desk shows a cabinet of highest quality. The serpentine drawer was a favorite design among Southern workmen, and much care was given to the making of the cabinet, while the exterior was often left very plain. The wooden knobs replace the original brasses. The desk was the property of one of the foremost leaders of Presbyterianism in Virginia in the middle of the eighteenth century. (Property of Union Theological Seminary).

PLATE V. CHIPPENDALE SECRETARY— WALNUT. (Georgia—c. 1760-1770). This carefully executed Chippendale secretary presents an interesting study in the cornice top. The term "broken arch" is often used erroneously to refer to the top shown on Plate VI. Notes made by a Charleston cabinetmaker of the third quarter of the eighteenth century reveal that Plate VI was known to him as a "scroll pediment," while the type illustrated in this plate was referred to as "broken arch pediment." The candle slides in the base of the top are a distinctive feature. The cabinet reveals a high type of workmanship. Secretaries of this type are, as a general rule, very tall. (Property of J. K. Beard).

PLATE VI. CHIPPENDALE DOUBLE-SWELL FRONT SECRETARY—MAHOGANY. (Virginia—c. 1760-1770). This exceptionally fine piece shows beauty in design and workmanship. The choice wood adds further to its charm. The double-swell front employed is sometimes known as the oxbow front. Although this is not a type found in quantity in the South, occasionally fine examples of such workmanship are discovered. This piece is believed to have been a part of the original furnishings of the Nelson House at Yorktown. (Property of Mrs. A. G. Ryland).

PLATE VII. CHIPPENDALE SECRETARY—WALNUT. (North Carolina—c. 1770-1800). This Chippendale secretary is unique. The arched door resembles the door of many cupboards found in Western North Carolina. The drop-front style is shown here as of a period before it became popular in the South. The fluted pilasters, and the inlay at the top add distinction to the piece. This secretary was made by John Wills, of Gaston County, for Zenas Alexander, who gave it to his wife Margaret at the time of their marriage; hence the initials M.A. in the rosettes of the scroll top. In 1826 Zenas Alexander bequeathed

this piece to his son, Robert Alexander, who at that time had his name inlaid across the top. Robert Alexander was the grandfather of the present owner. (Property of Odom Alexander).

PLATE VIII. TOP—HEPPLEWHITE SECRETARY-BOOKCASE—MAHOGANY. (Virginia—c. 1790). This is a winged bookcase. The center encloses a writing cabinet, and the general shape of the center is the same as illustrated in Plate XII, with the cupboards added at the sides. The tracery of the doors is an interesting feature.

PLATE VIII. RIGHT—HEPPLEWHITE SECRETARY—WALNUT. (Virginia—c. 1790). This piece of curly walnut shows the slant-top desk with the French feet and an interesting design in the doors of the bookcase top. Like many pieces found in the Shenandoah Valley of Virginia, it is made of curly walnut. (Property of Joe Kindig, Jr.).

PLATE VIII. LEFT—CHIPPENDALE DESK—MAHOGANY. (South Carolina—c. 1765). A slant-top desk of exceptional width, and made to order by Jacob Sass, of Charleston, in 1765. It is about five feet in width. Much furniture is found in Charleston attributed to Sass, and this desk is marked by him. In the Pringle House. (Property of Miss Susan B. Frost).

PLATE IX. SHERATON SECRETARY—MAHOGANY. (Virginia—c. 1780-1790). One of the finest American secretaries discovered. It was handed down for three generations by a family in Albemarle County. The eagle with shield and thirteen stars on its breast appear at the top. An inlaid eagle is shown on the roll top. The back of the desk and bookcase is paneled; the frame is Southern pine with poplar panels; the interior door has the initials L. B. burnt in; and the drawer linings are oak.

PLATE X. HEPPLEWHITE TAMBOUR DESK—MAHOGANY. (Virginia—c. 1790-1800). Much of interest attaches to this tambour desk, with French feet of the Hepplewhite style, and inlay, with carving. The carved shell of odd type is unusual. Tambour doors such as these which are often found in the South, on desks of fine workmanship, indicate that the product has been made in some furniture center. This tambour is secured by gluing strips of wood to a canvas or heavy cloth. (Property of Mrs. J. G. Hayes).

PLATE XI. TOP—HEPPLEWHITE TAMBOUR DESK—MAHOGANY. (Maryland—c. 1790). Desks of this type are found made in varying degrees of workmanship throughout the South. Some are finely inlaid with the bellflower design, and now command a high price. Some are found with a bookcase top.

PLATE XI. BOTTOM—HEPPLEWHITE DESK—WALNUT. (North Carolina—c. 1790-1800). Here the rural workman copied in native wood the finer type Hepplewhite desk. Desks with solid wood doors are frequently found. (Property of Ralph P. Hanes).

PLATE XII. SHERATON FALL-FRONT SECRETARY—MAHOGANY. (Maryland—c. 1800). This fall-front desk, a labeled piece, shows fine workmanship, and is of a type that was popular throughout the South. (Property of Mrs. W. W. Hubbard).

PLATE XIII. SHERATON FALL-FRONT SECRETARY — MAHOGANY. (South Carolina—c. 1800). This secretary is made in the same style as that illustrated in Plate XII, except that it shows the eagle inlaid pediment. The interior is of satinwood. Although rather large, it is finely made throughout, and in a large room in one of the old houses of Charleston its size is not apparent. (Property of Mrs. S. B. Pringle).

PLATE XIV. SHERATON SECRETARY—WALNUT. (Virginia—c. 1800). The workman here, under the influence of the designs of both Hepplewhite and Sheraton, tried his skill with native walnut. The piece is embellished with inlay, and ovals of flowers inlaid at the top of the legs. There is a cylinder top to the desk, with a slide that pulls out when the lid is raised. This writing slide has two wells for writing equipment. The spade foot is of Hepplewhite design. (Property of Mrs. F. B. Crowninshield).

PLATE XV. SHERATON SECRETARY—MAHOGANY. (South Carolina—c. 1810). Two views of a desk, as a means of showing the beginner that it is not always well to hold back on purchasing a fine piece because of its unprepossessing appearance. Top illustration shows "in the rough," in the parlance of the antique dealer, the product as it is found; the bottom illustration shows it as refinished. The replacing of the partitions in the doors was a small item, but the patches on drawer fronts were more difficult. This type of secretary is found throughout the United States, and was made in all sections. The handles, which do not show well in the illustration, have the eagle and thirteen-star design. (Property of Miss Lucy Stuckey).

PLATE XVI. EMPIRE SECRETARY— MAHOGANY. (Virginia—c. 1820). This type secretary was very popular in all the Southern states. Pieces like this are large and heavy, but the workmanship is of high quality. The lion's-paw feet are found on all types of Empire furniture along with the pineapple motif, as shown in the columns. The doors of this secretary are worthy of note. (Property of Mrs. Gabriel Cannon).

PLATE I

PLATE II

PLATE III

PLATE IV

PLATE V

PLATE VI

PLATE VII

PLATE VIII

PLATE IX

PLATE X

PLATE XI

PLATE XII

PLATE XIII

PLATE XIV

PLATE XV

PLATE XVI

XV

CUPBOARDS

THERE is no piece of furniture of the olden days around which more intimate associations clung, and to which more fond memories were wont to revert, than the old Southern cupboard. On every plantation there was some high genius from the colored quarters, constituted the particular guardian of the family cupboard, who saw to keeping it trim and clean, an old Mother Hubbard that went to the cupboard to get whatever might be wanted from the family store—sure of the supply, from ear muffs and hoods to some herb or toothsome dainty, and herself of a nature made for small confidences, to whom the children brought their troubles.

Although there is nothing which has retained about it more of the atmosphere of the home, the cupboard was, as a rule, often easily the most impressive piece in the house; and from the early sixteenth and seventeenth centuries showing fine decoration. Southern makers have not neglected their opportunities for refinement of the piece. The cupboard has received various designations, and it has been possible here to present a wide variety of types.

The earliest cupboard found in the South is the court cupboard. The word "court" coming from the French word meaning short, is accepted as referring to the carved-oak cupboard of the early seventeenth century. There are in America less than twenty cupboards of this type known. A cupboard, found in Virginia, illustrated in

this chapter, is stamped in style and construction as having been made very early; and it is safe to assume that as the Virginia workmen followed the English style of cupboard, that this piece was one of the first pretentious pieces made in the early settlement of Virginia, and, as far is can be determined, one of the earliest pieces of furniture found, made in the United States.

Following the court cupboard came the kas or kasse—1700-1740. Although the piece resembles the wardrobe as we know it, the piece is so large that it holds little appeal to the collector. A panel-door cupboard on a frame, with a cabriole leg, was made during this same period in the South, but examples are scarce, and are rarely found outside the Southern states. The open, pewter cupboard, the delight of many, is also found in the South, in Southern pine and walnut, made during the same period as the first-mentioned cabinets. Many have been found in the Piedmont section of North Carolina, and in the Valley of Virginia. They were used in inns and taverns as well as homes for the display of china and pewter, a vogue which, so lovely was it at that time, has returned at this day.

A unique type of cupboard found in the South, made during the Chippendale period, was that with the drawers at the base, and paneled, glass doors at the top. It was presumably a china press. This type is rarely found outside the states of Virginia and North Carolina. Standing, or wall cupboards, were made in Hepplewhite and Sheraton styles, but their number is so limited that it is useless to define their characteristics, as they had been superseded by the corner cupboard in these periods.

The corner cupboard, so much desired today, was introduced about 1710, and was changed to the moveable type in the 1750's. These are found in quantities throughout the South, ranging from the built-in type to the elaborate mahogany examples. The earliest specimens have the open top with shelves and paneled doors below. The sides of the top opening are scalloped in ogee scrolls, and the shelves are cut in design.

Some of the built-in cupboards made in Virginia and Maryland between 1730-1740, are very fine, with the shell top, although the workmanship varies. Often made by local or traveling craftsmen, the cupboard took the architectural features of the room in which it was built. The quality of the work was, in fact, often determined by the amount of money being put into the building of the house, or the cupboard. The moveable corner cupboard gave the maker further opportunity to display his skill, and to make a base and cornice more elaborate. Many fine examples in mahogany are found, and these were made with Hepplewhite and Sheraton characteristics, such as inlay and tracery. With the Empire period the corner cupboard was declared obsolete in style.

PLATES

PLATE I. TOP—COURT CUPBOARD—OAK. (Virginia—c. 1620-1630). Two views of a cupboard found in the vicinity of the first settlement at Jamestown. Ac-

cording to its style as compared with the English examples, it was made in the first quarter of the seventeenth century. The top, which is original and pegged, is of Southern pine, as is the interior lining. The drawer below the doors, one of the doors and the shelf in the base were missing. This is one of the earliest pieces made in America, and is believed to be the oldest piece of furniture of American origin. (Photograph, courtesy of J. L. Brockwell).

PLATE I. BOTTOM—COURT CUPBOARD—OAK. (Virginia—c. 1640). This old court cupboard has much about it which speaks for itself. It is of no moment to give space to a study of the type for the benefit of the average collector, as little chance stands out before him for such as it is. Such cupboards as are known, are rarely offered for sale, and those that are known are very few. This cupboard, originally from Yorktown, has an interesting history. It was removed to North Carolina during the Revolutionary War, and was owned by Isaac Collier whose wife, Anne Vines Collier, inherited it from her family. Her father, Thomas Vines, mentioned the cupboard in his will. Isaac Collier was a prominent colonial gentleman who had four sons in the Continental Army. One son, Myhill Collier, married Tabby Harrison, daughter of Benjamin Harrison, the Signer. The cupboard is believed to have been the property of Nathaniel West, brother of Lord Delaware. (Property of Mrs. J. L. Brockwell).

PLATE II. CUPBOARD ENCLOSING CHEST—PINE. (Virginia—c. 1680-1700).

This unique example shows the early wardrobe type of cupboard. There is a lid inside which encloses a chest or compartment which, we may be sure, made it generally useful. The paneling is of a peculiar type, and the decorative hinges are also out of the ordinary. The piece is massive, but not as heavy and impressive as it appears in the illlustration. A piece of this type offers little to hope for the collector, as it is rarely found.

PLATE III. QUEEN ANNE LINEN CUPBOARD—WALNUT. (Virginia—c. 1710-1740). This cupboard is very small compared to the general vein of cupboards as they appeared during this period. It encloses shelves which give point to its being used as a linen closet. Arched panels are seen, such as are found on pieces of this type made in the Queen Anne period. (Property of Charles Watkins).

PLATE IV. TOP—OPEN CUPBOARD—PINE. (Maryland—c. 1730-1750). Here is represented the open type of cupboard which was often called a pewter cupboard, due to the fact that it was made to hold household utensils, as indicated by the spoon rail. The sides are cut in ogee scrolls and the top is cut in decorative scalloping. The later cupboards showing this style, which are often very large and elaborate, and have paneled doors below with more elaborate base, are made of walnut. This is, however, a recognized example of pine open cupboards. (Property of Francis D. Brinton).

PLATE IV. BOTTOM—QUEEN ANNE

CUPBOARD ON FRAME—WALNUT. (North Carolina—c. 1730-1740). This Queen Anne cupboard of the early eighteenth century shows arched paneled doors that are particularly pleasing in design, and the cabriole legs are a distinctive feature. Due to its small size, this piece was used as a linen cupboard. It is a rare example of a little-known type of cupboard, found, as far as research and study has shown, only in the South.

PLATE V. CHIPPENDALE CHINA PRESS—WALNUT. (North Carolina—c. 1760). In this Chippendale china press, showing the Dutch influence, the tulip design is shown on each side of the eagle. The eagle holds the Masonic emblems in both claws. The designs are slightly raised, and carved. China presses of this general type are rarely found outside the South. From eastern North Carolina five pieces, carrying the same design on the cornice top, and with the scroll pediment, in mahogany and walnut, have come within the ken of this book. It it were possible to narrow down the field of search and locate the maker of this cupboard, the identity of some cabinetmaker of high ability in those distant days might be disclosed. (Property of Joe Kindig, Jr.).

PLATE VI. PANELED DOOR CUPBOARD—CHERRY. (North Carolina—c. 1780-1800). Although not constructed by a finished workman, much care was given to the decorative effect of the panels of this cupboard. Turned quarter-posts are inserted at the corners. It is one of three cupboards, exactly alike, found in the vicinity of Salem, and made from native cherry. It is a unique type, found only around Salem, remaining to us from Wachovian days, where craftsmanship, as descended from Ingebretsen and Feldhausen, was often fine. (Property of Ralph P. Hanes).

PLATE VII. CHINA PRESS—WALNUT. (South Carolina—c. 1780-1800). This local-made production of the Hepplewhite-Sheraton period, though a china press, still indicates the first shape, as such presses did until 1800. The Pennsylvania Dutch influence, which was carried with the settlers into South Carolina where the piece was found, is to be remarked. The inlay adds a distinctive feature along with paneling of the doors, which show the Sheraton influence. (Property of Ralph P. Hanes).

PLATE VIII. SHELL OR SUNBURST BUILT-IN CORNER CUPBOARD. (Maryland—c. 1730-1740). This type of cupboard is rare, although found at times in houses built around 1730 throughout the South. Frequently made by the builders of the house, as they show themselves to have been, and often of finer workmanship than the houses in which they were built, the indication is that they were the work of local cabinetmakers or traveling craftsmen. A paneled house in South Carolina containing one of this type of cupboard has been found, and while the surrounding paneling was of pine, the cupboard was of walnut and painted to match the wood. It must not be thought, however, that the cupboard was always a part of the original construction of the house. This cupboard

is one of high lineage, having come from the house of Colonel Tench Tilghman, on the Eastern Shore of old Maryland, dating as it does, to 1738. Colonel Tilghman is remembered as a member of Washington's staff, and the house in which the cupboard stood, was inherited by the Colonel from his grandmother. (Property of William B. Goodwin).

PLATE IX. CHIPPENDALE CORNER CUPBOARD—MAHOGANY. (North Carolina—c. 1770-1780). Again we find the eagle and Masonic emblem shown here with the ogee pediment, as it was called by early craftsmen, on a mahogany cupboard of fine quality from the same section as the china press illustrated in Plate V. The eagle decoration is identical with Plate V, but the cupboard has the finely scalloped shelves and a variation of the thirteen-pane door design, with eighteen panes shown here. The piece is made of fine mahogany. Features introduced advance the theory that the maker of these pieces was a very versatile worker. The scroll or vine-design on each side the eagle resemble the decoration on the cellaret in Plate III, Chapter XII. These pieces are all of exceptional type.

PLATE X. CHIPPENDALE CORNER CUPBOARD—WALNUT. (North Carolina—c. 1770-1780). This very large, inlaid walnut cupboard loses nothing from its excessive size. Inlay of rope design is shown in the ornamentation. The finials also show inlay. The arched door is a pleasing feature found on cupboards of this type. Some cupboards are of very generous proportions, but like this one, are so made that the beauty of line is not overcome by the unusual size of the piece. The piece was originally owned by General Joseph Graham, of Lincolnton. (Property of Mrs. Paul Chatham).

PLATE XI. TOP—CHIPPENDALE CUPBOARD—MAHOGANY (Maryland—c. 1765-1775). A mahogany cupboard of the finest type found in the South. The cornice top is particularly fine, with its band of carved fretwork below. The scalloped shelves, the pattern employed in the doors, and the choice of wood used on its lower doors all add to the distinction of this excellent piece. (Property of Joe Kindig, Jr.).

PLATE XI. BOTTOM—CORNER CUPBOARD—CHERRY (North Carolina—c. 1780-1800). Native cherry is used in this piece which has the stamp of fine workmanship upon it. The twisted-rope inset columns at the corners, the scroll top and

decorative door stamp it as something that could not have been done by any but an accomplished workman. It was made in the vicinity of Salem, and reflects the character of what was done by the many fine cabinetmakers that worked there during the latter part of the eighteenth century. The date of the piece shows it is late for Chippendale influence. (Property of Ralph P. Hanes).

PLATE XII. HEPPLEWHITE CORNER CUPBOARD—MAHOGANY. (South Carolina —c. 1790-1800). A finely inlaid and veneered cupboard showing the inlay as mentioned in Chapter XII, Plate VI. These cupboards show the thirteen-pane glass doors said to represent the thirteen original colonies. However, this design was used before the thirteen colonies came into being. Cupboards of this type show both Hepplewhite and Sheraton influence. (Property of Carroll H. Fowlkes).

PLATE I

PLATE II

PLATE III

PLATE IV

PLATE V

PLATE VI

PLATE VII

PLATE VIII

PLATE IX

PLATE X

PLATE XI

PLATE XII

XVI

CHESTS

SERVING many purposes and known by many names, the chest has always been an important piece of furniture. Its importance with the early settler has been stressed. Mentioned in the earliest inventories and in wills as early as 1647, with trunks, it must not be thought to have had to do with their origin. The less elaborate of the early chests were doubtless made here, but the finer "joyned chests," as they were known, were brought from England. Occasionally a locally-made chest of the finer type is found. The simpler ones were made of six boards, the side pieces forming the feet. Cedar, spruce, oak, pine, walnut, and swamp pine from the lowlands of the South, were employed.

The "joyned" or paneled chests were durably made, and presumably to hold valuables. They often had two locks, and were carved and stained. The 1650 type showed sides, back and front all paneled. Incised carving, known as scratch carving, in the shape of arches, containing conventionalized geometric or floral designs, was displayed on the front and sides. The tulip and sunflower were favorite motifs, and chests called by these names are found. Some examples had one long or two short drawers at the base; the stiles formed the feet.

Later examples show that the drawer became two long drawers, one above the other, both raised upon a frame. From this type comes the four-drawer chest, known variously as chest of drawers, nest of

drawers, and case of drawers. Another type which came into existence with the chest of drawers was a chest upon frame; and from this type derived the highboy with the six legs and stretcher frame, the legs of which, following Queen Anne influence about 1710, took the cabriole shape. Many chests of drawers made of pine and of walnut, in the South in the middle of

Empire chest-of-drawers

the eighteenth century, are found. Advertisements, as presented in the old Charles Town newspapers, are interesting in this connection.

Under Chippendale the chest of drawers took the serpentine curve in the front, and was popular. It remained in favor until after 1800. During this period the chest-upon-chest came into use. This, however, was not so much used as the highboy. Very few examples of either type are found.

In the Hepplewhite period the chest of drawers with the bowed front likewise prevailed, and the inlaid types are numerous. Many chests of drawers are found with the straight front inlaid in simple fashion, with French feet of Hepplewhite design. They were made in this style until 1810.

The type for chests of drawers, accepted as the American Sheraton, with three-quarter reeded columns at the corners, are rarely found. The Empire period brought many large and finely veneered pieces. Many were carved with the pineapple and acanthus leaf for motifs, but all of these are exceptionally large.

PLATES

PLATE I. TOP—CARVED CHEST—OAK. (Virginia—c. 1650). An oak chest with the conventional flower carving. The stiles, which are the upright pieces at the ends of the front, usually form the feet for such chests. This piece shows the early type of decoration and construction.

PLATE I. BOTTOM—DATED CHEST—WALNUT. (Virginia—c. 1796). A dated chest made for a member of the Wine family living in the Valley of Virginia. The date and the initials of the person it was made for are inlaid in the front. This type of chest was made from about 1730 to 1800. Earlier dated chests are found, but this is an example of a late period showing the overlapping drawer. (Property of William T. Sanger).

PLATE II. TOP—PANELED CHEST—WALNUT. (Virginia—c. 1700-1730). A completely paneled chest of a very rare type. Stiles form the feet here, as in the early chests. Round pegs are used as a forerunner of the hinge. There was a hole at the rear of each of the wooden end pieces underneath the top of the chest to which these pegs were fitted. The pegs were also attached to the back of the chest itself to form the hinge. (Property of Charles Watkins).

PLATE II. BOTTOM—CUPBOARD WITH CHEST INSIDE—PINE. (Virginia—c. 1710-1760). This piece, although of the cupboard type, has a chest with lifting lid inside. In the old inventories this type of cupboard was often designated as a chest instead of a cupboard. The iron H-hinges are visible in the illustration, and are of the type found on all types of earlier cupboards. (Property of Mrs. J. L. Brockwell).

PLATE III. TOP—CHEST WITH SLANT LID—WALNUT. (North Carolina—c. 1760-1780). An unusually interesting type. It has a number of small drawers in the interior, one of which is made of metal enclosed with wood. The height of this piece and the slanting lid make it available for writing purposes. The chest is marked, "Made by John Hobson," together with other writing not distinguishable. Other pieces have been found marked with the same name. As this cabinetmaker cannot be located as working in any one section, he is believed to have been one of the many traveling craftsmen. (Property of Miss Willie P. Garland).

PLATE III. Bottom—Chest of Drawers—Pine. (North Carolina—c. 1700-1730). A chest made of Southern pine, with the paneled end of the earlier type. The overlapping drawers indicate the date as being in the first quarter of the eighteenth century. The handles, which are original, are exactly like those found on the drawers of gate-leg tables. (Property of W. S. Ahern).

PLATE IV. Top—Queen Anne Chest of Drawers on Frame—Walnut. (North Carolina—c. 1740-1760). Numerous chests of this type have been found in North Carolina, and it is a style that was popular in the South. Some found have about half the number of drawers as the one illustrated.

PLATE IV. Bottom—Queen Anne Low Chest on Frame—Walnut. (North Carolina—c. 1740-1760). A rare type of low chest of fine quality.

PLATE V. Highboy—Cherry. (Maryland—c. 1700). A type rarely found complete, due to the fragile construction of the legs and under-stretchers. The legs have what is known as the bowl or cup turnings and onion feet. It has poplar drawer linings, and the back is Southern pine. (Property of J. K. Beard).

PLATE VI. Queen Anne Highboy—Walnut. (Virginia—c. 1730-1750). A scroll-top highboy of the plainer type, with the scrolls added to the flat top. The fan or shell decoration is often found on highboys of this period. All types of highboys

are rare in the South, and the finer made ones are rarely found showing Southern workmanship. These pieces are illustrated to show the different styles in various periods and not as a standard of excellence. (Property of Mrs. J. S. Archer).

PLATE VII. Highboy—Walnut. (North Carolina—c. 1760-1780). An inlaid highboy of a style peculiar to the outlying districts of the South. Not a finely executed piece, but one that presents certain interests, as it never has been finished. Part of the drawer fronts have not been pierced for the handles. (Property of Mrs. Paul Chatham).

PLATE VIII. Top—Chippendale Serpentine Chest of Drawers—Walnut. (South Carolina—c. 1770-1780). A type resembling the chests found with oxbow fronts. The date is indicated by the handles, although chests of this type were made earlier in the Chippendale period. (Property of Mrs. E. M. Crutchfield).

PLATE VIII. Bottom—Chippendale Serpentine Chest of Drawers—Mahogany. (Maryland—c. 1790). A fine veneered and inlaid chest with the inset fluted corners. It is Chippendale style, but the inlay indicates the Hepplewhite period. (Property of Mrs. Fred Sampson).

PLATE IX. Top—Hepplewhite Serpentine Chest of Drawers—Mahogany. (South Carolina—c. 1790). This finely inlaid mahogany chest of drawers shows the serpentine front with French feet. The matched veneered front is the work of a skilled craftsman. (Property of Mrs. J. G. Hayes).

PLATE IX. BOTTOM—HEPPLEWHITE SERPENTINE CHEST OF DRAWERS—WALNUT. (North Carolina—c. 1790). In this chest of drawers the local workman used native walnut, and cut the drawer fronts from the solid wood. The majority of four-drawer chests in walnut with straight front are found with solid drawer fronts. Walnut was rarely used as veneer, except on curved surfaces. The chest illustrated has only the inlay on the edge of the drawers instead of the bead, as in the chest at the top of the page. (Property of Carroll H. Fowlkes).

PLATE X. TOP—SHERATON SWELL-FRONT CHEST OF DRAWERS—MAHOGANY. (South Carolina—c. 1800). This chest of drawers in mahogany, with swell front, is of a type often designated as Hepplewhite, but Sheraton and Hepplewhite overlap so much in styles such as this, that it is best to refer to a piece of this type by the period in which it was made, as indicated by the handles, which are original. The inlaid fans in the French feet, and the center fan in the apron, are unusual. Chests of this

shape are found in quantity throughout the Southern states. (Property of J. K. Beard).

PLATE X. BOTTOM—SHERATON SWELL-FRONT CHEST OF DRAWERS—MAHOGANY. (Georgia—c. 1810). This type of the American Sheraton style is readily recognized. Chests of this type have a swell slightly flattened in the center. The reeded three-quarter columns at the corners are typical. Turned rosettes cover the posts at the top. This style of chest of drawers is often found with the front veneered with richly figured wood. (Property of J. K. Beard).

PLATE XI. SHERATON CHEST OF DRAWERS WITH ATTACHED MIRROR—MAHOGANY. (South Carolina—c. 1810-1820). This labeled piece is of a type rarely found, and is the first type of chest which appeared with mirror attached. William Rawsom is found listed in the 1819 directory of Charleston, one of the many operating as cabinetmakers when furniture making was coming under the Empire influence. He is supposed to be the son of the famous Joseph Rawsom, of Providence, Rhode Island. (Property of Francis D. Brinton).

PLATE I

PLATE II

PLATE III

PLATE IV

PLATE V

PLATE VI

PLATE VII

PLATE VIII

PLATE IX

PLATE X

RAWSON
AN ELEGANT VARIETY OF
FURNITURE,
CABINET WAREHOUSE,
No. 86 MEETING STREET
CHARLESTON, S. C.

PLATE XI

XVII

CHAIRS

NO ARTICLE of furniture is more easily placed in its rightful period by the study of its type than is the chair. No piece of furniture is harder to find at present than early chairs, particularly those of the first quarter of the eighteenth century.

The early seventeenth century chair, a seat of honor given to the lord or master of the house, has been shown in the wainscot chair presented, as typical. Until the first quarter of the eighteenth century, chairs were practically devoid of comfort, but with the decided change that came at the beginning of the century, curves took the place of straight lines, especially in chairs, and something better was provided.

The Dutch influence that came into England with William III is very noticeable in the early Queen Anne chairs, and to the Dutch is due the beautiful lines of those of the Queen Anne and Chippendale periods produced by English workmen. The Queen Anne influence produced the cabriole leg with different styles of feet, the majority in the South showing the pad foot. Due to the strength of construction, more examples of the Chippendale period are found than those of the last quarter of the eighteenth century. Richard MacGrath, of the period in South Carolina, it is recalled, was making carved chairs "with commode fronts and pincushion seats," and also described as "splat backs, with hollow slats."

Southern-made chairs of the Chippendale

leg, and claw-and-ball foot. The Hepplewhite chairs are easily distinguishable by period are rarely found with the cabriole

Top—Seventeenth century turned chair
Center—Turned chair known as a carver chair
Bottom—Turned chair of Dutch influence

159

the shield-shape back which, along with his heart-shape, largely predominate, and some have been found showing fine inlay and carving. The Sheraton period produced many chairs with square backs in the neo-classic style, which were very fragile.

Along with the chairs influenced by the master designers, we find the turned chairs made in quantities for use wherever finer chairs could not be had. Many Windsor chairs, heretofore thought to have been solely a product of the New England and Middle Atlantic States, have been found in the South, of Southern manufacture. A. Redmond, in the *South Carolina Gazette*

Painted Sheraton or early Empire Chair
Empire side chair

and General Advertiser, in 1764, advertised "Turnery in all its branches," and "Likewise Windsor chairs, either armed or unarmed, as neat as any imported, and made of much better stuff." It is strange to note that some are found with a great variety of woods used in their construction, while some are found made completely of walnut; and two writing-arm Windsors made entirely of walnut were found in the South.

Nothing is more difficult to place in a definite manufacture than a chair, as only certain deviations from a general style will help to do so. Many sets of chairs were made in the South for the original furnishings of homes, and these only can be definitely placed. It has been said that one can tell American-made chairs of the Chippendale period by the fact that the side seat rails have a tenon that passes through the rear legs, but this cannot always be used to determine a Southern-made chair, as many of the workmen learned their trade in England, and did not follow this construction.

PLATES

PLATE I. WAINSCOT CHAIR—OAK. (Virginia—c. 1620-1640). The wainscot, which harks back into the early days, is of unusual interest. The fact that this chair is made of American oak establishes it as a Southern chair, as do the facts that two chairs and a part of a third were found within a radius of forty miles in Chesterfield County; and that no others of this type with the square legs, rasp-turned at the top, have been found in the United States, lead us to the inference that it was not imported from some other point. This type of chair in England is generally ascribed as being made in the first quarter of the seventeenth century. (Property of William B. Goodwin).

PLATE II. TOP—TURNED CHAIR—WALNUT. (South Carolina—c. 1700). A unique chair of early derivation, in which the turnings follow those found on gate-leg tables. This chair presents a problem as to its identification by the student of furniture, as it follows no well-known type. There may have been some kind of covering for the back. It is of little need to say anything here except to show that the workman often employed his own ideas in the furniture he made.

PLATE II. BOTTOM—TURNED CHAIR—WALNUT AND CHERRY. (North Carolina—c. 1750-1760). Much interest attaches to this turned chair, thought to have been one made as part of the original furnishings for the Moravian Church, established in Wachovia about 1753. Its date is later than appears at first glance, as shown by the splat in the back and top rail. Attention is particularly directed to the seat of the chair, as raised above the seat rails, and made on a frame with turned stretchers extending from the extension of the turned legs to the back and between the legs in front. (Property of the Misses Pfhol).

PLATE III. TOP—TURNED CORNER CHAIR—WALNUT. (South Carolina—c. 1700-1730). This turned chair shows the modified Spanish front foot, and is unusual in having the square stretchers in base.

PLATE III. BOTTOM—WRITING-ARM WINDSOR CHAIR—WALNUT. (Virginia—

c. 1760-1780). This represents a rare example of the Windsor chair, only two of which have been found to date, which are the only ones surviving, according to well-known authorities. The two chairs are finely turned, and both are made of walnut. Chairs of any type with writing arms are rare. These were found in the vicinity of Richmond. (Property of Joe Kindig, Jr.).

PLATE IV. TOP—QUEEN ANNE SIDE CHAIR—WALNUT. (Virginia—c. 1720-1740). The Dutch influence is distinctly shown in this chair. In the Queen Anne period, American chairs followed the style of the chairs brought from England. The shape of the leg was directly from the later William and Mary chairs. (Property of J. K. Beard).

PLATE IV. BOTTOM—QUEEN ANNE CORNER CHAIR—WALNUT. (Virginia—c. 1720-1740). This type of chair is often called a roundabout chair. An unusual type, with the deep scalloped skirt. The roundabouts appear among the Chippendale chairs along with the fiddle-splat back, ladder-back and ribband chairs, but are not generally so popular. (Property of J. K. Beard).

PLATE V. TOP—CHIPPENDALE LADDER-BACK CHAIR—MAHOGANY. (North Carolina—c. 1760-1775). Here is a fine type of side chair, delicately carved and having the sunk or hollowed seat. The piercing of the cross rails in the back is typical of this type of chair, but the delicate carving is unusual. (Property of Mrs. Paul Chatham).

PLATE V. Bottom—Chippendale Side Chair—Mahogany. (South Carolina—c. 1760-1775). This chair back is very similar to one illustrated in Chippendale's plates. It is in line with his ribband-type back. Although this chair does not show the carved ribbon effect, the scroll and shape are very similar. From the home of the Pickens family. (Property of Mrs. Paul Chatham).

PLATE VI. Chippendale Side and Corner Chairs—Applewood. (Virginia—c. 1780). These side and corner chairs are of much interest, owing to the fact that they were made by a local or journeyman craftsman at work on the Virginia plantations. Native wood is here used to great advantage. These two chairs are part of a set of ten side and two corner chairs made as part of the original furnishings for Oakland, an old manor house on the James River, in Cumberland County. This entire set has been largely preserved but, like other sets, has become separated in pairs or otherwise. (Property of J. Pope Nash).

PLATE VII. Chippendale Armchair—Walnut. (North Carolina—c. 1760-1770). This extremely large armchair reflects the work of a chair builder with a taste for good proportion. The shape of the back is excellent, showing the cut-out splat that was very popular, and used throughout this period, and employing a derivation of the fiddle-shape back of the Queen Anne period.

PLATE VIII. Hepplewhite Shield-Back Chair—Mahogany. (Virginia—c. 1790). This is a Hepplewhite chair exhibiting Adam influence. It shows a back shape found on many American Hepplewhite chairs, which is more the form of the heart than that of the shield. It is one of a set of chairs thought by many connoisseurs to be one of the finest known sets of the present day. The set, however, is distributed among members of the family which formerly owned it. (Property of Mrs. E. D. Hotchkiss, Jr.).

PLATE IX. Top—Sheraton Chair—Mahogany. (Virginia—c. 1795-1800). Here is a Sheraton-style chair, with typical square back, ornamented with carving in low relief, the arrow motif used by Adam, and adapted to chairs by Sheraton. These are found in sets used in a dining room or hall. Few are found throughout the South. (Property of Mrs. J. G. Hayes).

PLATE IX. Bottom—Sheraton Side Chair—Mahogany. (Georgia—c. 1800). This plain Sheraton side chair follows the finer chairs in design, but is devoid of carving. It shows the slip seat often found in chairs of the Chippendale period. The square, tapered legs and stretchers are found on most American Sheraton chairs. (Property of Mrs. Fred Sampson).

PLATE X. Windsor Armchair—Mixed Woods. (Virginia—c. 1785). This and the labeled Windsor, in Plate XI, do not present the finest type of this style chair. They do, however, present evidence that these chairs were made in the South. The fact that William Pointer is listed in the 1782 census of Richmond, and that the capital was moved to Richmond in 1782, helps place the date of this chair, although little else is known of the man. (Property of J. B. Watkins).

PLATE XI. WINDSOR CHAIR—MIXED WOODS. (Virginia—c. 1785). This Windsor chair shows the shaped top piece and the saddle seat. Mr. Pointer has been cited as having a partner, but no further information is to be offered, except that Crouch's Tavern is spoken of in Mordecai's *Richmond of Bygone Days*. (Property of G. F. Scheer).

PLATE XII. WINDSOR CHAIR—MIXED WOODS. (Virginia—c. 1790). This Windsor presents the label of Andrew and Robert McKimm, of Richmond, and is of a type all of which show heavy, turned spindles in the backs, but good saddle seats and well-turned legs. Robert McKimm is among those listed as a chairmaker in the first census of Richmond. Aside from the label on the chair, nothing further is known of Andrew McKimm. (Property of Mrs. A. G. Ryland).

PLATE XIII. WINDSOR CHAIR—MIXED WOODS. (Virginia—c. 1820). A late Windsor chair and rather crudely made. The turned, back supports and legs have what is known as bamboo turnings. This type of chair was made in great quantities. The labels in this, and in Plate XII, have been retouched to bring out the lettering. (Property of B. F. Powell).

PLATE XIV. TOP—QUEEN ANNE WING CHAIR—WALNUT. (Virginia—c.

1720-1740). Wing chairs of quality are rare in all periods, although many are found, crudely made. (Property of Mrs. E. M. Crutchfield).

PLATE XIV. BOTTOM—CHIPPENDALE WING CHAIR—MAHOGANY. (South Carolina—c. 1760-1780). A chair of the later type, and a style in which the majority of chairs of this style are found. (Property of Mrs. Gabriel Cannon).

PLATE XV. TOP—CHIPPENDALE SOFA—MAHOGANY. (Virginia—c. 1760-1780). A Chippendale style sofa having the tapered legs, indicating the latter part of the period. The scroll arms and curved back are typical of the period. (Photograph, courtesy E. Steinmetz).

PLATE XV. CENTER—HEPPLEWHITE SOFA—MAHOGANY. (Virginia—c. 1790). A sofa having Hepplewhite and Sheraton motifs combined. It is possibly English made. (Property of Mrs. J. G. Hayes).

PLATE XV. BOTTOM—HEPPLEWHITE SOFA—MAHOGANY. (Maryland—c. 1790). An excellent piece and nicely inlaid. Hepplewhite sofas are very rare in the South.

PLATE XVI. TOP—SHERATON SOFA—MAHOGANY. (South Carolina—c. 1800). A sofa of the better type, with the legs at the frame inlaid with panels.

PLATE XVI. CENTER—SHERATON SOFA—MAHOGANY. (Virginia—c. 1800-1810). A late Sheraton sofa with Empire influence. The style becomes heavier in these later pieces.

PLATE XVI. BOTTOM—EMPIRE SOFA —MAHOGANY. (South Carolina—c. 1820). An elaborate sofa in which the carving is of fine quality. The Dolphin feet and shell in back are exceptionally well done. (Property of J. B. Griffin).

PLATE XVII. SHERATON PAINTED SETTEE—MAHOGANY. (Maryland—c. 1810). A marked settee of fine quality in the late Sheraton style. The scenes are supposed to represent local landscapes. (Property of Mrs. Rush Sturges).

PLATE I

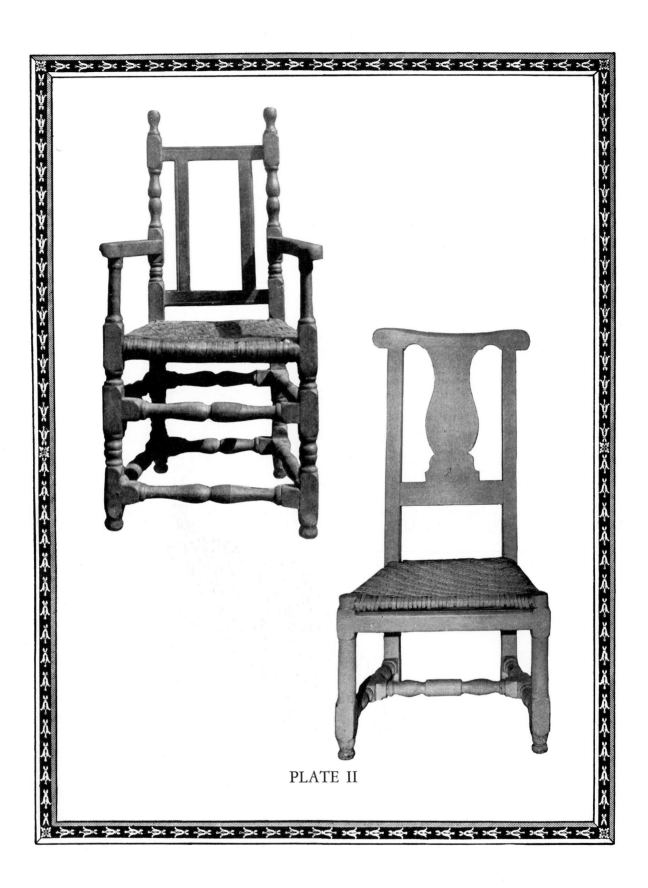

PLATE II

PLATE III

PLATE IV

PLATE V

PLATE VI

PLATE VII

PLATE VIII

PLATE IX

WINDSOR CHAIRS,

Made and Warranted by

WILLIAM POINTER,

In the neateſt manner, and may

be had at his ſhop, between

rouch's Tavern and the *Go-*

vernor's House — RICHMOND

PLATE X

WINDSOR CHAIRS
Made and W anted by
Pointer & Childres
And may be had at their *fhop* be-
een Crouch's Tavern and the
Go nor's Houfe, RICHMOND.

PLATE XI

Andrew ⅔ ----- llum
makes
WINDSOR ----rs
In the neateſt and b---- manner at ---- our
Chair ſhop near
RICHMOND.

PLATE XII

ALL KINDS OF
WINDSOR CHAIR
MADE & SOLD, WARRANT
BY
SEATON & MATTHEWS
BELO
SYCAM   REET,
PETERSBURG.

PLATE XIII

PLATE XIV

PLATE XV

PLATE XVI

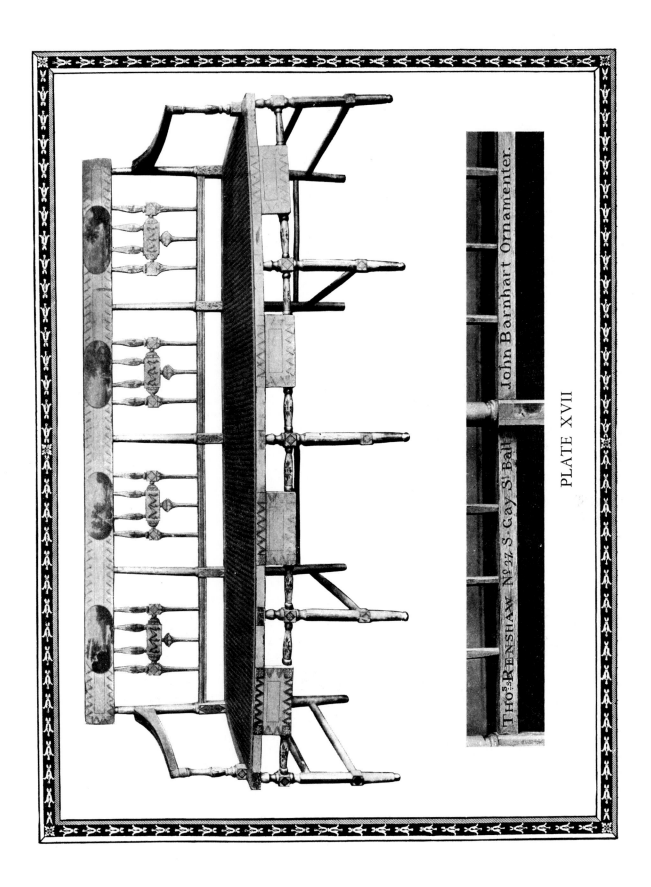

Tho.ˢ Renshaw Nº 27 S. Gay Stᵗ Balt John Barnhart Ornamenter.

PLATE XVII

XVIII

BEDS

IT IS a well-known fact among collectors that there are no Southern bedsteads before 1700 to be found, but despite the failure of the beds to reveal themselves, no one disputes the fact that they were made in number. Inventories mention bedsteads and couches as local-made as early as 1659, but no bed of that date has survived to tell the story of what they were. An old bed of 1720-1740 is, however, presented. This scarcity of early bedsteads has been explained by the fact that they could not be utilized by the owners for making any other piece of furniture when discarded, and were doubtless done away with.

A study of conditions leads to the belief that early Southerners, as a rule, contented themselves with simple beds, although a few of the more costly carved oak beds were brought from England, but once conditions had improved, many Southern beds began to take on fine airs and lend themselves to decoration. Following the middle of the seventeenth century, Virginia gentlemen of high estate, when they could, sought their slumbers amidst draperies of much magnificence, as consorted with their dignity in manner and dress. Many spent lavishly for furnishings of a bed. The inventory of the estate of Colonel Epes, Henrico County, Virginia, in 1670, lists: "Feather bed with camlett curtains and double vallins lind with yellow silke, bolster pillow, counterpane, rodds and hooks, tops and stands, one curtaine and some fringe." Costs were more than twenty-five

pounds. The bedstead is not mentioned. Beds were of first importance, and it was customary, during the early periods, when going on an extended visit, to take one's bed.

Some of the early bedsteads were built in the wall or placed in a niche in the wall,

Chippendale bed fully draped

with two carved posts on the outside, the other two posts being plain. However, the greater number of beds had four elaborately carved oak posts, with a paneled and carved headboard. Some of them contained cupboards in themselves. Examples are known to have secret cupboards at the head to conceal weapons.

Wooden cornices, employed up to 1750, gave way to the valence, and the four-poster was in vogue. The draperies were to continue through the century, with the patriots of the Revolution sleeping in four-posters richly draped, but the tendency from then on toward more lightness, until 1800, when draperies were omitted.

As a rule, the majority of the beds that have been collected had plain headposts. Not until the Sheraton period do we find all four posts with carving. Headposts before this time, hidden by the draperies, were nearly always square, tapered posts. Fine Hepplewhite and Sheraton examples have been found. Beds of unusual beauty are shown in this book, one showing reeded posts and spade foot. The Empire beds were enormous, some with posts eight inches in diameter and nine feet tall; and in the early part of this period, some were elaborately carved with the leaf and pineapple motifs.

PLATES

PLATE I. QUEEN ANNE BED—WALNUT. (North Carolina—c. 1720-1740). A particularly fortunate find is represented in this piece, one of the earliest American beds found. While not one of the most beautiful of early American beds, it surpasses in interest many of those excelling it in the matter of good looks. No bolts are used in its construction, and it was held together with rope. The measurement of such beds, head to foot, was usually about six feet, and the mystery is as to how sleep was induced within such restricted limits. The type of foot used in the bed resembles the mule-foot. Octagonal posts, as shown here, are also found on later pine beds. This bed was found near Bath, and was at one time a part of the equipment of the home of one of the state's oldest and most representative families. (Property of J. K. Beard).

PLATE II. HEPPLEWHITE BED—MAHOGANY. (South Carolina—c. 1780-1790). In striking contrast to the old walnut bedstead is this finely carved and inlaid Hepplewhite bed, showing the reeded post and spade foot, typical of the period. Beds of such high quality as this were usually made with canopy top; but in most cases, due to so many of the beds having changed hands the tops, as a rule, have been discarded. In beds such as this, a top mattress was laid on a second feather-filled mattress, placed next to slats, which fulfilled, in some uncertain way, the purpose of the modern springs. The headposts of such beds were usually hidden and were plain in style until the period of Thomas Sheraton. This bed was found in South Carolina, where many such beds have been discovered, most of them, however, with the posts cut off and being used for other purposes. (Property of J. K. Beard).

PLATE III. SHERATON BED—MAHOGANY. (South Carolina—c. 1800). This Sheraton bed carries the turned headposts. The spade foot is discarded in favor of the reeded and turned feet, which were usually bound with brass. The leaf carving is still found on the finer beds of this period. This is one of two beds, identical in workmanship, although one is slightly larger than the other. (Property of Mrs. T. C. Gower).

PLATE IV. EMPIRE BED—MAHOGANY. (Virginia—c. 1820). This bed of the

Empire period is shown with the original tester of carved wood, which has been gilded. The hands, holding the rings at the corner, is a unique design. The pineapple, signifying "plenty in the home," which appears at the top of the posts, was used extensively on Empire furniture. The spiral twist, introduced as a motif at this time, was used on posts of beds, and was found on the legs of furniture. Leaf carving of a coarser type is found in this period. (Property of J. K. Beard).

PLATE V. Top—Sheraton Bed—Mahogany. (North Carolina—c. 1800). An exceptionally fine bed of a late type.

The carving is of high quality. There evidently was an arched canopy on this bed. (Property of Joe Kindig, Jr.).

PLATE V. Lower Left—Empire Dressing Table—Mahogany. (South Carolina—c. 1820). An elaborately carved dressing table carrying all the outstanding characteristics of the period.

PLATE V. Lower Right—Sheraton Washstand—Mahogany. (South Carolina—c. 1800). Washstands appear in this shape from 1760 to 1810, taking the characteristics of the period.

PLATE I

PLATE II

PLATE III

PLATE IV

PLATE V

XIX

MISCELLANEOUS PIECES

PLATE I. Tall Clock, Sheraton Period—Mahogany. (Virginia—c. 1790-1800). A clock of fine workmanship, and marked on the face "John M. Weidermeyer, Fredericksburg." No information is available concerning this man, but if he was a cabinetmaker he deserves recognition, as a study of the case will show. Cabinetmen often made cases, but imported the works. (Property of Carroll H. Fowlkes).

PLATE II. Piano Case—Mahogany. (Maryland—c. 1810). A fine piano case marked "L. Ricketts, Baltimore." The author has never seen better carving of its type, even on pieces from Phyfe's workshop. The case is veneered with bird's-eye maple and mahogany on mahogany. L. Ricketts is listed in the Baltimore directory of 1810 as working there as a cabinetmaker. (Property of Mrs. Paul Chatham).

PLATE III. Upper Left—Cupboard—Walnut. (North Carolina—c. 1800). Students of furniture design who like the modernistic type, should study this illustration. The maker came close to being more than a century ahead of his time. The outstanding half-round containers are partitioned for bottles.

PLATE III. Upper Right—Sheraton Sideboard—Walnut. (South Carolina—c. 1810).

PLATE III. Right Center—Desk—Walnut. (North Carolina—c. 1790). A desk with a fine interior and inlaid drawer fronts of fruitwood. (Property of F. B. Priest).

PLATE III. Left Center—Chippendale Drop-Leaf Table—Walnut. (North Carolina—c. 1750-1770). Showing a table with somewhat different type of foot.

PLATE III. Center—Chippendale Chair—Walnut. (Virginia—c. 1760-1780).

PLATE III. Lower Left—Sheraton Sideboard—Maple. (South Carolina—c. 1810). A sideboard of curly maple with inlay.

PLATE III. Lower Right—Chippendale Corner Cupboard—Walnut. (North Carolina—c. 1740-1760). Fine architectural type of cupboard from North Carolina, where many of this type are found.

PLATE IV. Upper Left—Chest-of-Drawers—Walnut. (North Carolina—c. 1770-1790). This chest has a carved eagle in the skirt. Chests of this type, with different decorations and feet, are found in quantity throughout the South. (Property of Miss Willie P. Garland).

PLATE IV. Upper Right—Cabinet—Mahogany. (Virginia—c. 1820). A small cabinet evidently to house a collection of books or for display of trinkets. (Property of J. B. Ferneyhough).

PLATE IV. CENTER—SHERATON CELLARET—MAHOGANY. (Virginia—c. 1800). An inlaid cellaret with turned legs of a shape peculiar to those found in the rural districts. (Property of Mrs. E. M. Crutchfield).

PLATE IV. LOWER LEFT—CHIPPENDALE ARMCHAIR—WALNUT. (North Carolina—c. 1770). A country-made chair like many found. (Property of Mrs. E. M. Crutchfield).

PLATE IV. LOWER RIGHT—QUEEN ANNE LOWBOY—WALNUT. (Virginia—c. 1750). Lowboys are so rare in the South that they are not described in the text. However, some are found. (Property of Mrs. J. G. Hayes).

PLATE V. UPPER LEFT—CHIPPENDALE-PEMBROKE TABLE—MAHOGANY. (South Carolina—c. 1760-1775).

PLATE V. RIGHT—CLOCK—CHERRY. (North Carolina—c. 1790). A small clock made in the shape and style as tall clocks, and called grandfather clocks for this reason. It was found in Salem, and is an exact duplicate of a tall clock found there. The case has a remarkable grain. Small clocks of this type are very rare. (Property of Ralph P. Hanes).

PLATE V. LOWER LEFT — CHEVAL GLASS—MAPLE. (South Carolina—c. 1800). A rare type of the early Empire period. It has brass-paw feet. (Property of Joe Kindig, Jr.).

PLATE VI. MANTELS. Two fine mantels from old Southern homes. The top one has the eagle and shield carved from solid wood. The lower mantel is from Montmorenci, a magnificent home in North Carolina. It has the applied decoration.

PLATE I

PLATE II

PLATE III

PLATE IV

PLATE V

PLATE VI